JUANITA SIMPSON

Walking the Waves

GOD'S GUIDING HAND IN MICRONESIA

CHRISTIAN • LITERATURE • CRUSADE
Fort Washington, Pennsylvania 19034

CHRISTIAN LITERATURE CRUSADE

U.S.A.
P.O. Box 1449, Fort Washington, PA 19034

GREAT BRITAIN
51 The Dean, Alresford, Hants., SO24 9BJ

AUSTRALIA
P.O. Box 91, Pennant Hills, N.S.W. 2120

NEW ZEALAND
10 MacArthur Street, Feilding

ISBN 0-87508-324-2

Copyright © 1998
Juanita Simpson

This printing 1998

All Scripture quotations, unless otherwise indicated, are taken from the New International Version © 1973, 1978, 1984 by International Bible Society. Used by permission of Zondervan Publishing House.

PRINTED IN THE UNITED STATES OF AMERICA

To
my dear father
who introduced me to Jesus

Contents

PREFACE

*H*ave you ever wondered how it felt to Peter that day he stepped out of the boat onto the waves? Did it feel hard and smooth under his feet like marble? Or was it soft, wet and squishy—like walking through a swamp or marsh? Maybe it was more like balancing on columns of air.

When I was young I was just daring enough to wish that I could try walking with Peter, just to feel the exhilaration of that moment. I have not yet attempted to step out of our Mission boat onto the surface of the azure Pacific, but I have experienced the exhilaration Peter must have felt that day.

There is nothing more thrilling and life-changing than hearing the voice of God.

And He is still speaking! To hear Him speak is a moment of transcendence . . . a walking on the waves!

INTRODUCTION

I realize that it is a dangerous thing to write a book of this type today. Movies and television have encouraged fantasizing when life becomes difficult or downright boring. In addition, there are many counterfeit prophets and false prophecies abroad.

Because our hearts are deceitful (Jer. 17:9) we may create fantasies to solve problems of identity, using our imaginations to create a "reality" that we desire. If we are committed Christians, it is possible for us to fantasize about "what God has said to us." It is dangerous to begin with a strong desire and then look for Bible verses to confirm it, because they can always be found! Going to Scripture with a bias may lead to self-delusion. Some try to validate Scripture or God's will by feelings. It's important to be discerning of our own evil and selfish lusts. We must ask ourselves, "Is this just my selfish desire, or am I willing to accept from God whatever He has planned, even if it goes against my personal longings?"

What is even more serious about fantasizing is that it has the potential of opening our minds not only to self-deception but to demonic deception. Many times the enemy will merely mirror our hidden desire or subconscious wish, putting into words what we find difficult to admit to ourselves. We must be astute students of God's character, God's principles, and God's revealed Word. For example: If a "revelation" in any way runs counter to the holiness of God, or contradicts His principles regarding sexual and marital relationships, or requires a distortion of Scripture to support it, it becomes evident at once that we have not heard God but, instead, some other voice. "God deals only in truth and will not participate in deception."[1]

I believe that one of the primary sources of fantasies and counterfeit prophecies is our unwillingness today to live with our situation, no matter how difficult. We seem to be searching for an easy way out, and if we are Christians, we want to manipulate that escape route so that it appears to have the sanction of God. Pride and the desire for power may be the underlying motivation of those manipulations. We must learn to live with life's realities, no matter how unpleasant. "Spirituality is to be lived out in the grime of everyday rugged reality."[2] A study of the lives of God's most faithful servants in Scripture and history will reveal this characteristic. But in our day of television "sitcoms" it seems that we have lost the value of facing and dealing with reality in the God-ordained ways. False fantasies and counterfeit prophecies are rooted in rebellion against a God who often chooses to use sickness, hardship, pain and death to mold us into the image of His Son, who knows all about those things! (Rom. 8:28–29; Heb. 4:15; 5:8).

Our lust for instant Christianity and the easy life may cause us to fall prey to lying prophets, even as the Jews did in the time of Jeremiah and Ezekiel when the fall of Jerusalem was imminent. Counterfeit prophets fill people with false hopes. They speak visions from their own minds—not from God's mouth—and assure the unrepentant and proud that all is well: God will bless them (Jer. 23:16–17). How did they become false prophets? Jeremiah 23:18 gives us the source of the problem: they did not stand in God's council, being immersed in God's Word, paying the price of deep and serious study with a humble, attentive spirit. **They wanted a quick fix!**

The Lord says about these false prophets: *"I did not send these prophets, yet they have run with **their** message. I did not speak to them, yet they have prophesied."*—Jer. 23:21. They are like counterfeit ambassadors who might claim to represent President

---

[1] Ron Susek, *The Fatal Fantasies of Women;* to be published.
[2] Ibid.

Clinton and the U.S.A. They speak for a person and a country without the proper credentials and with a deceptive message arising from their own or Satan's delusions. They say, "I had a dream . . ."—but dreams can come from God, demons or indigestion! They prophesy the delusions of their own minds (Jer. 23:25–26). What does God think about these so-called prophets who declare, "The Lord said . . ."? He is *against* them because they claim to represent Him when He didn't send them (Jer. 23:30–32).

How can we be sure that we are hearing God and being His true representatives? We must stand in His council (Jer. 23:22). We must follow and proclaim His Word faithfully. His Word *alone* has the power to change lives; it is grain, not straw. Grain is heavy and nourishing. Straw is flimsy and has no food value. God's Word is also fire—destined to purify gold and consume straw. It is a hammer—able to break a hard heart, or to crush one that refuses to be broken (Jer. 23:28–29).

The Lord's Word reminds us: many false delusions will abound (Matt. 24:11, 24; 2 Peter 2:1–3); we must wisely test the spirits (1 John 4:1); we must diligently watch and pray (Matt. 26:41); we must be filled with the Holy Spirit and the Truth (Eph. 5:18; John 14:6).

Today we often hear: "The Lord said to me . . .", "I saw a vision . . .", "I had a dream . . .", "The Lord told me to tell you . . .", "I'm going to prophesy . . .", "I got a word from the Lord. . . ." I, too, have heard the Lord speak, as well as having seen visions and dreamed dreams. Most of the time it has been for my own personal guidance, growth or comfort. Many of those revelatory words and sights I have never divulged to anyone. Some were intensely personal. What I write about here I do with the utmost humility and in response to the urging of the Lord and godly advisors. My only purpose is to be obedient to my Father and to further His cause in the lives of His people.

I don't know exactly how the Almighty God spoke to the prophets, priests and kings of long ago. But I do know how He speaks to me today! In God's Word we read that sometimes men were spoken to from a burning bush, by an angel, by a donkey, in dreams, or in visions. But many times the Scripture only says, "The word of the Lord came to . . ." or "By the word of the Lord a man of God came. . . ." Did they hear the Almighty speak in audible tones, or did the Holy Spirit reveal something to them inwardly? I don't know! I just know that the God who revealed Himself to them in crystal clear words has not changed. He is the same personal Father today who delights in revealing Himself and His will to those who are listening.

We have a great advantage over the men and women of the distant past because today we hold the very Word of God in our hands. We also have the promise of the Savior that, if we belong to Him, the third Person of the Trinity, the Holy Spirit, will speak the words of the Father to us (John 16:12–15).

I believe that in our time the Lord speaks primarily through His Word which we can read. However, we often treat the Bible as a history book or a text on theology instead of being attuned to "hear" the voice of God "speaking" to us. As far as I know, I have never heard the audible voice of God, but I am not sure. There have been times when His revelation was so personal that I didn't know afterwards whether I had heard with my ears or only with my heart. The more important thing was that I knew I was in the presence of a *personal, speaking* God.

There have been other times when I was not at the moment reading the Bible and yet I knew the Holy Spirit was speaking a very precise message to me from the Father. Because I am, as a missionary, fully conscious of the world of "other spirits" at work, I do not lightly accept a message like this, because I am aware of the warning of John that we need to *"test the spirits to see whether they are from God."*—1 John 4:1. The primary "testing tool" in our arsenal is God's revealed Word, the Bible. If the message we hear in any way contradicts the inspired Word or the character of God, we can be certain that it is *not* spoken by the Holy Spirit of God.

INTRODUCTION

It is my custom, when I believe that the Holy Spirit has spoken inwardly or that I have received a specific message from the Lord out of His Word, to ask Him to confirm those thoughts so that I cannot be led astray by some other "voice." I have found the Lord wonderfully faithful to confirm His messages to me since it is *His desire* that I continue to walk in His way and do His will. His will, of course, is found in His infallible Word. Anything which I suppose to be the will of God that is not consistent with His character is a deception originating in my own self-delusion or Satan's imposed delusion.

We must not, I stress, allow the excesses and deceptions which abound today to deter us from the sincere pursuit of God and the commitment of our lives to hear His voice.

In the years since I began "walking the waves" with the Lord in this exhilarating and extremely personal communication, I have frequently been asked certain questions. The most common is: "How does this happen? Do you just close your eyes, open the Bible, and point?" The answer to that one is: NO! I have never done that. Most often when there is a decision to be made or a question in my mind that needs an answer, I simply pray and wait for the answer. It usually comes in the portion of Scripture that I am studying, although not necessarily at that precise time. It may not come quickly, but when it is there I recognize it. "There is a fullness of faith that comes from the Holy Spirit when something is from God."[3] Sometimes the Lord speaks out of the "clear blue" when I haven't even asked Him, or am not aware that He is leading along certain lines. *Paramount to being spoken to by the Lord this way is our personal, diligent study of the Word and our commitment to do His will at any cost.*

A second question is one that I am sometimes asked by theologians: "But aren't you taking that verse out of context?" I have been a serious student of the Word for fifty-some years. Context is very important to me. I always do my utmost to understand the circumstances surrounding the verse or verses

---

[3] Ron Susek, op. cit.

which I am studying. I believe that with God's help I ordinarily *"correctly handle the Word."*—2 Tim. 2:15. My response to this question is very simple, as all my theology is: *God has the privilege of taking His words out of context if He chooses.* I don't! But if He wishes to say something out of Scripture that is different or unexpected, I think He has the perfect right to do that! As an example: It was the Holy Spirit who took the words spoken to Ahaz in Isaiah 7:14 and applied them to Mary and Christ.[4] We must be careful that we are not careless interpreters of the Holy Word of God. Every new thought must square with the rest of God's revealed Word, and with His revealed character.

I have committed my life to the inerrancy of the Word of God. It is my practice to believe and accept whatever I read in Scripture as absolute truth to live by! I don't always understand how all the parts fit together, but that is no problem for me. I refuse to manipulate any passage to make it agree with some preconceived theology. If I cannot explain a seeming paradox, I assume that the cause is my finite mind, not God's infinite Word! One of the prerequisites to "hearing the voice" of God is faith to believe that God is still speaking today from His living Word—and the desire to hear and obey whatever He says! Another is to allow God to be God!

I believe that the Lord can and does speak to us from every part of His Book. For this reason, it has been my habit for years to begin at the beginning in Genesis and systematically study Scripture through to Revelation. I have no idea how many times I have done this, but I do know that every day as I study His Word, God reveals something new or reviews something important that I have forgotten. I prefer not to set a limit on the amount I cover at a sitting, in order to give the Holy Spirit freedom to speak at length on one or two verses if He chooses. Sometimes He speaks through a whole book all at once.

I am reminded of an experience I had many years ago in

---

[4] *"Therefore the Lord Himself will give you a sign: The virgin will be with child and will give birth to a son, and will call Him Immanuel."*

INTRODUCTION

Palau. I was reading through the Bible and had come to Leviticus! I approached my devotion time with a bit of dread. I took it to the Lord in a rather whiny prayer: "Lord, do I *have* to read this? I need to sense Your presence and get close to You tonight!" Now of course I didn't *have* to read Leviticus that night. I had the whole Bible from which to choose! But it seemed as though the Lord was challenging me to try Him—to discover whether the whole Bible is really His Word from which He can speak.

At 3 A.M. my daughter Angela woke up to find the kerosene lantern still burning. "Mother, are you still awake? What's the matter?" she queried.

"Everything's O.K., hon. I'm just reading the book of Leviticus."

That night I spent six hours reading through the entire book of Leviticus and worshiping the Lord in it! Again and again I found the reminder: "*I AM THE LORD!*" Coming to the full realization of who He is led me to bow in adoration before His very presence, with tears for His beauty and my failures. Since that day I have expected God to speak through every portion of the Bible.

I am confident of the inerrancy of the original manuscripts, but I have also found that the Lord is perfectly capable of speaking through various translations and versions. I do not believe that all translations are equally viable, but I am amazed at how His voice speaks even in spite of possible human error! I began my spiritual pilgrimage with the King James Version, and used only that for many years. In more recent years I have been blessed through the New International Version. God has spoken very clearly to me at times from the Amplified Bible, the Living Bible, and from the Palauan translation of the New Testament and Shorter Old Testament, as well as from other translations and paraphrases.

I believe that the Lord still uses many methods to reveal His will and His thoughts to us. He is not bound by our finite minds or our limited understanding of His ways. However, the most precise and straightforward form of communication that we know is *talking*. God, the Almighty Communicator, is still "talking"! While we may experience God's greatness and power through the earthquakes, the winds and the fires, and He may use them to get our attention, He speaks primarily in a *"gentle whisper"* as He did to Elijah (1 Kings 19:11–13). It is His desire to lead us deeper and higher than we have ever experienced before—not for our delight only, but for His glory and the achievement of His will on earth through us!

1

A CLOSED BOOK OPENS

"Remember the word unto Thy servant, upon which Thou hast caused me to hope. This is my comfort in my affliction: for Thy word hath quickened me."—Psa. 119:49–50 (KJV)

*T*he voice of the little Palauan deacon was choked as he read the words in his own language. It was Friday morning, September 8, 1967. We had gathered in the chapel of Bethania High School in the Palau Islands for our morning devotions, but the atmosphere was somber. My husband had been missing for two days!

As an islander, the deacon knew chances were slim that John would be found. But the Lord and I both knew he would *not* be found alive on this earth. He had slipped through a watery grave into the arms of the Captain of his soul, just as the Lord had told me he would six years before! Yes, I already knew.

Yet, that painful morning, it was the Word of God that *"quickened me"* to hope as I remembered some of the promises He had made—for John, for me, for the children, and for His work in our beloved Micronesia. I had learned several years earlier that *"God is not a man, that He should lie . . . hath He said, and shall He not do it?"*—Num. 23:19 (KJV).

This whole thrilling adventure had begun the day I realized that God wanted to speak to me personally through His living Word, the Bible. I had believed in Him and trusted His Word for years, but I had not till then expected Him to speak directly to *me*, Juanita Simpson, an individual living in the

NOW of our twentieth century world!

Born in 1928, I grew up in Connecticut, occasionally go-ing to church and sometimes longing to know that man named Jesus. But it was only when the bottom dropped out of my world that that faint longing became a desperate need!

I came home from elementary school one day to discover that my mother was not home. That was not unusual. Mother was often gone for several hours, taking care of an elderly lady or doing some sewing for the wealthy people in whose garage-house we lived. When Mother didn't show up that night, however, I began to worry. When I asked about her, Dad mumbled something about her "taking care of someone."

The next day I once again quizzed my father, "Where is Mommy?" I sensed that something was awry when he changed his story, saying that she was visiting one of her sis-ters in another state. How could I understand that my bro-ken-hearted father could not bring himself to tell me the pain-ful truth?

I did not hear the real story or know the ramifications of what had happened until I went back to school on Monday. There my "friends" taunted me with, "We are not *your* friends any more! We saw the story in the newspaper. You come from a *bad* family!" Walking home alone that day, I tried unsuc-cessfully to hold back the tears. Losing mother and friends in one day was more than I could face. So began a very painful and lonely period of time for this eleven-year-old turning twelve.

Each morning my father and brother left the house early to travel downtown—my father to work and my brother to high school. Later I got up by myself; dressed and tried to fix my long hair acceptably; ate a scant breakfast; and walked alone the several blocks to school. At noon I walked home to a silent house; turned the radio on loud to "Helen Trent," try-ing to drown out the silence and my thoughts; and ate a bowl of soup.

My father, who had recently rededicated his life to the Lord after years of wandering, began to take my brother and me to church. One of the special memories I have of that hard time was the comfort and encouragement I received as the three of us gathered in the living room some nights for "Family Devotions." My dad had taught us to play horns, as he did, so we would play and sing hymns together. He would then read something from the Bible and we would kneel and pray. The Lord deeply touched my grieving heart during those precious times.

One evening as we knelt to pray, Dad said to me, "Wouldn't you like to accept Jesus as your Savior?" I didn't know what he was talking about, but not wanting to hurt his feelings, I concurred. He then led me in a prayer which I repeated after him. I didn't understand what I had done or if I had done anything. But from that time on I began to listen attentively in church. I reasoned that if this thing called salvation was so vital to my father that he would talk to me about it when it was not his habit to talk about personal things, it had to be important! I needed to find out what it was all about.

I had lost faith in the entire human race and had vowed that I would never trust anyone again. However, after a month or two of learning about the Lord, I came to understand that Jesus wanted to be my Friend. His reassuring words *"I will never leave thee, nor forsake thee"* (Heb. 13:5b, KJV) gave me hope in the midst of despair. Perhaps He could be trusted. I hadn't thought much about my sin before that, but I was then able to face the truth of Romans 3:23 [1] and rejoice in the forgiveness of 1 John 1:9. [2] In my extremity I turned my whole life over to Jesus, and found in Him deliverance from the burden of sin and comforting arms of love to encircle this lonely little girl.

Many years later, in 1966, I wrote to my father from 9000 miles away, in Palau: "Daddy, I want you to know something that I have often thought about but never told you. Hardly a week goes by that I do not thank the Lord that you cared enough for me to lead me to Him. I have always been well

---

[1] *"For all have sinned and come short of the glory of God."* (KJV)
[2] *"If we confess our sins, He is faithful and just to forgive us our sins, and to cleanse us from all unrighteousness."* (KJV)

aware of the fact that you did not have to keep me and raise me, and how can I thank you for that? I know that it was difficult for you, but where would I be now if you had not loved me?. . . I have felt for many years that I have a deeper fellowship in the Spirit with you than with anyone else I know.

"I don't know why I'm writing all of this to you today, but I'm thankful that the Lord has given me this quiet Sunday afternoon to say what I have thought so many times. I just want you to know that you are one of the dearest on earth to me."

Soon after my conversion I began to investigate this mysterious book called the Bible. I found it indeed strange and hard to understand. For a while I would read avidly, and then would quit, discouraged by my lack of comprehension. Finally in high school I developed a fairly regular habit of reading, and so I started at Genesis and read through to Revelation. The Book began to open its closed doors to me, and I found it full of wonderful truth, as well as pointed references to my failings!

My teenage years were not easy. My father had remarried and my brother had taken off on his own. My stepmother, though a Christian, was on quite a different wavelength from mine. My independent spirit and Rhoda's lack of experience in raising children caused us to run head on. When Rhoda gave birth to Janet it took off some of the pressure, but then I was relegated to the position of baby-sitter. I truly loved Janet, and her brother Steve when he came along, but found myself becoming less and less attached to my home.

I was 16 and a junior in high school when I determined that it was time to plan my future. I needed to think about what I should do with my life. I decided that I could analyze myself better than anyone else could, so I should figure out what I was capable of and enjoyed—and go for it! My self-analysis showed that I probably could make a good teacher. I reasoned that if I were going to teach, I would want to teach subjects that I enjoyed. Then and there I chose my vocation: I would be a teacher of Bible, music and math.

During my high school years I was attending and helping in a small church where the gospel was preached and the needs of the world were emphasized. It seemed that more often than not, I came home from a service feeling guilty. I had found the only true Friend in the world and He had changed my life, but what about all those others who had had no chance to know about Him yet? I was deeply convicted about my lack of concern for other people's souls as I meditated on verses like John 4:35 [3] and Matthew 28:19–20. [4] I finally realized that I had no right to plan my own life, since I had given it to the Lord. Hadn't He said in Proverbs 3:5, *"Lean not unto thine own understanding"*? When I left the choice with Him, I knew that He wanted me to be a missionary.

With great misgivings I was able to finally answer "Yes" to this call from the Lord to serve Him on the mission field. I somehow felt that He was spoiling all my well-made plans, and that I would never get to do what I knew I could do best. Twenty years later I remembered that difficult decision and laughed! I was sitting in my open classroom at Bethania High School in the Palau Islands, waiting for the girls while wiping the ever-present perspiration from my brow. Suddenly I remembered that day and praised my all-wise heavenly Father. There I was—a missionary teacher teaching math, music and Bible! The girls slowly coming to their desks wondered why their teacher was chuckling out loud to herself. It was a good opportunity to help them know more about a great and personal God who can be trusted to plan our lives.

The best place I could think of to prepare for missionary service was Providence Bible Institute, so that's where I headed after graduation from high school. As a freshman I was asked to give my testimony. After telling briefly of my

---

[3] *"Say not ye, 'There are yet four months, and then cometh harvest'? Behold, I say unto you, 'Lift up your eyes, and look on the fields; for they are white already to harvest.'"* (KJV)

[4] *"Go ye therefore, and teach all nations, baptizing them in the name of the Father, and of the Son, and of the Holy Ghost: teaching them to observe all things whatsoever I have commanded you: and, lo, I am with you alway, even unto the end of the world."* (KJV)

conversion, I explained that God had called me to be a missionary. I told them that I was willing to go anywhere and do anything, *except be a pastor's wife!* This produced some snickers, which was my purpose in saying it. But actually I was dead serious. If anyone thought that I was willing to be some congregation's dartboard, they could think again!

It wasn't long before I had to "eat" my words. John Simpson, whom I had loved for three years, came home from the Navy and began attending Providence Bible Institute. It was wonderful being there together, but his goals were set on the pastorate and mine were not! I finally had to swallow hard while agreeing to be a pastor's wife. What a poorly prepared missionary I would have been if God had not led me through that "wilderness"!

2

Testing God's Will

"I will instruct you and teach you in the way you should go; I will counsel you and watch over you. Do not be like the horse or the mule, which have no understanding but must be controlled by bit and bridle or they will not come to you."—Psa. 32:8–9

After John and I were married we often needed to know the Lord's will regarding some decision, and yet somehow He had to almost drag us to the right place at times. I think we were like the mule in Psalm 32. One such incident took place when we moved from Rhode Island out to Indiana after two years of marriage.

Never having been that far "west," we were rather awed at our own courage while inwardly quite frightened at the undertaking. Consequently, we prayed much about a place to live while we were at Taylor University. We told the Lord how much we wanted to know and do His perfect will. With this prayer on our hearts we entered the university housing office.

"Could you suggest some place where we might live?" asked John. "Would you have anything available here on campus?"

"Well, I don't think so, but let me check the records," answered the man at the desk. Having leafed through several folders, he suddenly turned, saying, "Say, you're really fortunate. We have just one place left—and it's on campus!"

Thrilled at this evident leading of the Lord, we followed him across campus to view our new home. "Well, here it is" were the words that burst our balloon into a million pieces.

We tried to seem undecided so as not to hurt his feelings. Then we started apartment-hunting in the nearby towns and cities. After all, we reasoned, nobody could possibly expect us to live in that shabby little old trailer left from World War II. Why, the thing had a leaky roof and an ice box! As if adding to the insult, you had to walk about half a block (or so it seemed) to use the "community" bathroom and shower. Certainly we could find something better than *that*!

The following three months we learned a graphic and costly lesson. The first month we lived in a lovely upstairs apartment in Marion, a city ten miles from the university. By the end of the month we had worn thin our meager finances and bodily stamina traveling back and forth, and were happy to move into a little garage-house we found just four miles from school. It was perfect . . . until the weather turned cold and we couldn't keep our hungry heating-stove fed. Finally, having recognized the limitations of our budget, we turned to a new and very clever idea. We would share a small house with another couple. All went well until John typed a term paper late one night when they were tired . . . and shortly afterward I was sick one day on the living room couch which was our bed!

Back to the office we went like puppies with our "tails between our legs," humbly asking in hushed tones if there might possibly be something—just *anything*—on campus. There was only one place open, we were told. We went out to look at it, retracing our steps all the way up to the very same trailer door. "We'll take it!" we shouted in unison.

It was Christmas, so we set up our tiny tree at the end of the trailer and settled in for one of the happiest and most peaceful holidays of all our Christmases together. We felt badly that we had wasted so much time and money, but grateful that we had learned that the Lord really does know best and that our job is to pay better attention.

The following year we answered the call to a little church planted in the middle of a cornfield. While serving that church we were given a direction by the Lord that we didn't even recognize for several years. John was discussing missions one day with a Mission Secretary of a well-known denomination. The lady was quite disdainful as she let him know that we would not be considered because of our evangelical position. When pressed, she finally admitted that if we went through all sorts of education and fund raising we might at some point be acceptable to them. Desiring to insult us, she made it clear that "our type" would be suited to only one of their fields. Asked what field that was, she answered, "Micronesia." And the reason given was that "the Micronesians are simple people."

We had never heard of Micronesia before. When John asked her where this strange-sounding place was, she responded, "Oh, it's a bunch of tiny islands in the western Pacific." Looking it up later, we found that Micronesia is the name of one of the three large divisions of islands in the Pacific Ocean, along with Melanesia and Polynesia. At that time most of Micronesia was included in the U.S. Trust Territory of the Pacific, an area entrusted to the United States by the United Nations at the end of World War II. The U.S. was the fourth country to have control of most of Micronesia, with Spain, Germany and Japan having preceded us there. We decided that it was well named when we found that the approximately 2100 islands in Micronesia are so tiny that the total land area is smaller than Rhode Island even though they are spread over an ocean area equal in size to the continental United States!

It is amazing what the Lord can do through an insult! That day we fell in love with the "simple people" of those tiny islands who just longed to know the Father who longed to adopt them into His family. We knew that the Mission Secretary was right about "our type fitting in." We were simple people too, whose only desire was to lead others to the Father. During the next eight years we thought often of those island people whom we had never seen, and prayed that the Lord would send true messengers to them so that they would someday come to know Him.

Another time we came very close to making a wrong decision which could have been far more serious than our earlier missteps. We had served for four years in our little pastorate in Powers, Indiana. They had been blessed, fruitful years in which the church had grown in many ways in spite of our mistakes. But the time had come to leave. We knew the Lord wanted us to move on, but we didn't know where He wanted us to go.

Several churches had written to us. After having considered all of them, we felt drawn to two different ones. We prayed, but could find no answer to our dilemma. Should it be Wingate or Darlington? We decided to do the sensible thing —use our heads. We sat down and weighed the two churches in the balance.

"They both have about the same attendance and membership," John observed.

"Yes," I agreed, "but Wingate has a nicer parsonage, don't forget."

"That's true. I don't think there's too much difference in the church buildings, though, do you?"

"No, I guess not. Of course, money is not one of our considerations, but Wingate did offer a larger salary," I reminded.

"The scales seem to tip slightly in favor of Wingate, don't they," John said thoughtfully.

"Well, of course the really important question is: Which church would be most receptive to the gospel?"

"Yes," John agreed with a sigh. "If only we could know that!"

"Well, how can we?" I shrugged.

"All right then, let's go with the sensible choice. I'll get the paper and typewriter and dictate the letters we think we should write to the two churches," John said decisively.

That night I slept soundly for a few hours. Then I woke up. I tossed and turned, wondering why I couldn't go back to sleep. Our second child was due in a month, and I wondered momentarily if she had decided to arrive on the scene early. Dismissing that thought, I tried again to sleep, but without success.

I began to pray. After I had prayed for a few minutes, I realized that I wasn't making any headway in my prayer because my mind was filled with only one question . . . so, I asked it.

"Lord, why am I awake?"

Immediately into my thoughts came the answer, "Because there is something important for you to think about."

So that was it. I tried to think of important things. Probably in the matter of two or three seconds my thoughts turned to two signed, sealed and stamped letters on the kitchen table waiting patiently for early morning mailing.

"Did we make a mistake, Lord?" I asked, knowing the answer. "But we tried our best to make the right decision," I complained.

The Lord really didn't need to remind me of something I knew so well from past experience. "Your reasoning powers, no matter how sound they seem, are not sufficient to make decisions on matters about which *I alone* can know the outcome."

"But, Lord," I persisted like a whining child, "we wanted to know which church would be most receptive, and had no way of finding out."

In my mind's eye I suddenly saw a letter we had received from a member of the Darlington congregation a couple of weeks earlier. He had written, "There are many in our church and community who need to be born again. I believe that the Lord will use you here if you accept the call."

"Forgive us," I pleaded. "You gave us the answer two weeks ago, but we didn't accept it as guidance from You. Help us to trust Your leading and recognize Your answers from here on. Tomorrow morning we'll tear up those letters and write two new ones." Whereupon, I turned over and fell asleep at once.

Another step in the right direction came four years later in the Darlington church. Outwardly, things were going very well. Attendance and interest were up. New buildings and organizations had been started. But we knew well that all of this apparent success was only a candy shell over a primarily empty spiritual work.

Had we, after all, made a mistake in coming to Darlington? Had all of our efforts been wasted? Was it hopeless? Would we have to give up—a failure—to let someone else take over all our hopes and dreams for spiritual awakening in this church?

As these ideas ran rampant through our thoughts and conversations, we received a letter of invitation to candidate at a large church in the West. It sounded like all that we wanted the Darlington church to become. Wouldn't it be wonderful to pastor a church like that? We took the letter before the Lord and asked Him if this, then, was our answer.

The next day I read on my knees, *"And let us not be weary in well doing: for in due season we shall reap, if we faint not"* (Gal. 6:9, KJV). We realized that our weariness had caused us to be looking for greener pastures when we needed to continue in our well doing where God had placed us. We praised the Lord together for His clear leading through the infallible Word. [5]

Exactly two months later the Lord used a visiting evangelist in our church to turn it upside down. The "due season" had arrived. It was the beginning of three years of fruit-bearing which the Lord alone had been able to see ahead of us.

Thus far I had learned many things about seeking the Lord's will. I had found that He wants to lead us if we will let Him. He always knows what is best for His children. He often shows us His will through deep convictions of the heart or through circumstances, but most often through His Word. My feet, however, were still on the safe, solid ground of complacent Christian living. I had not yet learned to walk on water.

---

[5] See principle #1, Appendix.

3

A Discovery Changes My Life

"Step out on the waves that would crush you!
Step out in the storm that would hush you!
And you will find as you touch the crest
You feared so much, and walk on its breast,
There was One walking there, the whole night through,
Walking, watching, waiting—FOR YOU!" [1]

The Vision Lives [2] was the title of the book. For some unknown reason, the author, Ben Pearson, had sent us a copy. Finding that it was the biography of Charles and Lettie Cowman, I decided to read it. We had been interested in the Oriental Missionary Society for years, and particularly in recent months as the Lord had been speaking to us about His work in distant places. The Cowmans had founded the O.M.S., and I was curious.

"Mr. Pearson may be a wonderful Christian but he certainly is a poor writer" was my first reaction to the book. Looking back, I can only be thankful for Ben Pearson's faithfulness in writing and sending me the book that has so greatly influenced me! The story of the Cowmans' missionary work in Japan was inspiring, but when I came to the middle of the book and Charles Cowman died, *The Vision Lives* was set aside. "What could there possibly be left to tell about a woman in her sixties?" I thought. "I'm not going to waste my time read-

---

[1] Mrs. Charles E. Cowman, *Springs in the Valley;* Grand Rapids, Michigan, Zondervan Publishing House, 1996 (originally Cowman Publications, Inc., 1939), p. 30.

[2] Publisher unknown; believed to be out of print.

WALKING THE WAVES

ing the rest."

They were arrogant words, which I have lived to regret now that I find myself at that same age. But there was something from within compelling me to pick up that book again. It was in the second half that I made the discovery that has changed my life!

I read in amazement that Mrs. Cowman expected the Lord to talk to her personally from His Word. And even more surprising was the fact that HE DID! I found to my astonishment that the Lord spoke to her about all kinds of decisions—small and great. He even gave her special messages for others . . . like the time He directed her to tell Emperor Haile Selassie, then an exile in England, that he would be restored to his kingdom in Ethiopia. The message was right there in black and white on the pages of the Bible.

As I thought about this and other unusual experiences in Mrs. Cowman's life, I tried to analyze the difference between her life and mine. I was mature enough by then to know that all of us, after all, are mere human beings. I felt that what one woman could do in the spiritual realm ought to be equally available to others. I took a careful look at myself before the Lord and recognized for the first time that the major hindrance in my life was a simple thing: I didn't have the faith of Lettie Cowman.

"Lord, I want that kind of faith, too," I pleaded. "From now on, I want You to speak to me like that. As I read Your Word, I am going to *expect* You to say something directly to me. And I promise that I will believe that You said it, and will act on it. Unworthy as I am, I want to be another Lettie Cowman, or Moses, or Abraham, because You are my God just as You were theirs." [3]

Thus began the thrilling adventure through whose chapters I have flown since. That very same evening, November 12, 1961, the Lord put my new faith to a startlingly severe test.

John and the children had gone to bed. I sat alone in the

---

[3] See principle #2, Appendix.

living room, my Bible in my lap. I was thinking about how during the past two years the Lord had been drawing us closer and closer to missions. I remembered that day seventeen years before when I had told Him that I would be a missionary if that was what He wanted. But John had felt called to the pastorate, and I had obeyed the Lord in His request for me to serve as a pastor's wife.

I recalled the times during those intervening years when I had wept a little with longing to be the missionary God had called me to be. "I just don't understand, Lord. I know that You told me I should be a missionary, but here I am, a pastor's wife, probably for the rest of my life. What's going on?"

I always felt a bit guilty during those moments. Since I had rebelled at first about the thought of serving in the pastorate, when I longed for the mission field it seemed as though the old rebellion had not been settled. Invariably I felt the need to apologize to my Father. "I'm really sorry, Lord. You know that I am willing to do whatever You have planned— even if it means spending the rest of my life as a pastor's wife."

But way down deep there was an indefinable something that often brought tears to my eyes when I read a book, heard a message, or saw slides of missionary work. Hearing then the gentle whisper of the Lord, "All in My time; I will take care of everything," I would then go on my way, happily serving where He had put me.

In spite of all this preparation, I somehow seemed totally unprepared for the question I felt the Lord was asking me that night. "Suppose I should tell you that the time has come to be a missionary. If I were to ask you tonight to serve Me the rest of your life in Micronesia, what would your answer be?"

The shock of this thought coupled with the nearness of His presence threw me to my knees by the couch. There I stayed for hours—I don't know how many—as I read my Bible, prayed, listened, and wept. I am not sure to this day if the Lord's voice was audible or not. I do know one thing for sure. As the Lord and I communed together, I felt the pressure of a physical hand on my shoulder!

A question had been posed which was awaiting an answer. Looking back now and summarizing my answer, I see that it was filled with "buts." "Lord, You know that I am more than willing to be a missionary . . .

"BUT . . . we're too old now to make the necessary adjustments.

"BUT . . . mission boards don't accept you when you're over thirty.

"BUT . . . John is not linguistically inclined—he'd never be able to learn a new language.

"BUT . . . our children are both in school already. Where would they go to school in Micronesia?

"BUT . . . who would support us?

"BUT . . . how would we get there in the first place?

"BUT . . . we don't even know a mission board to apply to.

"BUT . . . what about our belongings?"

All my "buts" seemed to bring only one challenging response from the Lord. Each one He answered in exactly the same way: **"Don't you trust Me? Where is your faith?"**

I finally admitted that all my "reasons" had to *melt like wax at the presence of the Lord of the whole earth."*—Psa. 97:5 (KJV). How could I be in the very presence of the Almighty and not trust Him? *"With Your help I can advance against a troop; with my God I can scale a wall."*—Psa. 18:29.

Having faced and dismissed all these questions by simple faith in a great God, I finally found the courage to voice the one real "reason" why the whole idea was absolutely impossible. The Lord and I both knew that it had been the one thought present in my mind from the beginning of our communion together.

Eyes brimming over with tears and lips quivering, I questioned, "But, Lord, what about John's *heart trouble*? You know missionaries can't go to the field sick. The doctors have told him he will have to slow down or give up the pastorate. How could he ever be a missionary?"

It was then that the Lord gave me the first of many unusual promises. In thinking of the faith of Mrs. Cowman, I had been reading earlier the "faith chapter," Hebrews 11. The Bible lay before me on the couch, open to this chapter. Looking down, I could just make out through tear-blinded eyes, the twelfth verse: *"Therefore sprang there even of one, and him as good as dead, so many as the stars of the sky in multitude, and as the sand which is by the sea shore innumerable."* (KJV).

The Lord whispered to me, "You're right about John's health. He's 'as good as dead.' But even this doesn't hinder Me. If you will just trust Me, I will bring forth fruit through his life that you can't even count."

I had asked to have a faith like Abraham's. Now I thought about that great man's faith. All alone in a foreign land, without a child of his own, he nonetheless believed God's fabulous promise simply on the basis of his faith in the character and power of God. *"He staggered not at the promise of God through unbelief; but was strong in faith, giving glory to God; and being fully persuaded that, **what He had promised, He was able also to perform.**"*—Rom. 4:20–21 (KJV).

I remembered the words often quoted to me by my father: "Expect great things of God! Attempt great things for God!" As I pondered the omnipotence of our God, I realized that we cannot expect anything too great *from Him* nor attempt anything too great *for Him* when He is leading us on.

Oh, the unutterable joy and release that filled my entire being as I said, "Yes, Lord." In that simple answer rested the commitment of my all to Him. Then, in came the peace that can come only through complete abandonment to the will of God.

Rejoicing in the warmth of His smile of approval, I read on in Hebrews 11, substituting in my thoughts the words of which the Lord reminded me.

"By faith 'John,' when he was come to years, refused to be called 'a well-known pastor and evangelist'; *choosing rather to suffer affliction with the people of God* 'in Micronesia' *than to enjoy the pleasures of* 'home' *for a season; esteeming the reproach of Christ greater riches than the treasures in* 'America'; *for he had respect*

unto the recompense of the reward. By faith he forsook 'America,' *not fearing the wrath of* 'relatives and friends'; *for he endured, as seeing Him who is invisible. By faith they passed* 'over' *the* 'Pacific Ocean' *as by dry land. . . . By faith the walls of Jericho fell down, after they were compassed about seven days.*"—Heb. 11:24–27, 29a, 30 (KJV).

I wondered what the *"walls"* were, and if *"Jericho"* was all of Micronesia or only part. I realized that the only way to *"compass"* all of Micronesia was in prayer. "It took them seven days," I thought. "I wonder how long it will take us? Seven years, perhaps? Or much longer?"

4

MY QUESTIONS ANSWERED

"Call to Me, and I will answer you and tell you great and unsearchable things you do not know."—Jer. 33:3

*I*t seemed as though years had passed since earlier that same evening I had agreed to put this verse into practice, expecting the Lord to answer when I asked. Now I rose from my knees and started toward the bedroom, walking on an unseen cloud—or was it water?

I stopped short in the middle of the kitchen floor, and my thoughts landed with a thud back on solid ground. Knowing myself very well, and being somewhat familiar with that old father of liars, I called out once again to the One who is the Truth.

"Lord, tomorrow morning when my feet touch the cold planks of the floor, the Devil is going to say, 'Did you ever have a fantastic dream last night! Well, you can forget it right now. You know perfectly well it's impossible, so just go on about your business and don't even admit to John that it happened. He'll only laugh at you anyway. How silly can you be!'

"Right now I know it's not a dream, Lord, but maybe I'll doubt it in the morning. I want You to do something for me. In the next few days, as doubts or questions arise in my mind, I want You to give me the answers *out of Your Word*. Be so specific that I will have complete assurance within a few days that this is Your call to Micronesia. Then I will never again doubt the veracity of it."

For the next three or four days, I asked and He answered.

WALKING THE WAVES

Sometimes the answer was given as I had my personal Bible study. Sometimes it came into my mind in the form of a verse I had memorized long ago. Some of the answers were in our daily devotional book, *Streams in the Desert*,[1] which we read at the table each morning; or it was the verse one of us selected from our box of "Daily Bread" verses.[2]

My question: "Is John's work really finished here?"
His answer: *"And he could there do no mighty work, save that he laid his hands upon a few sick folk, and healed them. And he marveled because of their unbelief."*—Mark 6:5–6a (KJV).

My question: "What will happen to us when we get so far away from home?"
His answer: *"If I take the wings of the morning, and dwell in the uttermost parts of the sea; even there shall Thy hand lead me, and Thy right hand shall hold me."*—Psa. 139:9–10 (KJV).

My question: "Is it really worthwhile to go to those scattered islands where there are so few people?"
His answer: *"Go ye into all the world, and preach the gospel to every creature."*—Mark 16:15 (KJV).

My question: "Should we go as soon as possible or wait another year or two?"
His answer: *"I must work the works of Him that sent Me, while it is day: the night cometh, when no man can work."*—John 9:4 (KJV).

My question: "Suppose we can't even do the work when we get there?"
His answer: *"Verily, verily, I say unto you, 'He that believeth on Me, the works that I do shall he do also; and greater works than these shall he do; because I go unto My Father.'"*—John 14:12 (KJV).

My question: "But we might not have the wisdom to deal with the Micronesian people. What then?"

---

[1] Mrs. Charles Cowman, *Streams in the Desert*; Grand Rapids, Michigan, Zondervan Publishing House, 1996 (originally Cowman Publications, Inc., 1925).
[2] See principle #3, Appendix.

His answer: *"If any of you lack wisdom, let him ask of God, that giveth to all men liberally, and upbraideth not; and it shall be given him. But let him ask in faith, nothing wavering."*—James 1:5–6 (KJV).

My question: "Will we be safe living in Micronesia?"

His answer: *"And who is he that will harm you, if ye be followers of that which is good? But and if ye suffer for righteousness' sake, happy are ye: and be not afraid of their terror, neither be troubled."*—1 Peter 3:13–14 (KJV).

My question: "We're getting older. Will we have the stamina to do the work?"

His answer: *"They that wait upon the Lord shall renew their strength; they shall mount up with wings as eagles; they shall run, and not be weary; and they shall walk, and not faint."*—Isa. 40:31 (KJV).

My question: "Will we have enough to eat?"

His answer: *"The Lord is my shepherd; I shall not want."*—Psa. 23:1 (KJV). *"Who satisfieth thy mouth with good things."*—Psa. 103:5a (KJV).

My question: "Will we go through life with no land or house—nothing to call our own?"

His answer: *"Ask of Me, and I shall give thee the heathen for thine inheritance, and the uttermost parts of the earth for thy possession."*—Psa. 2:8 (KJV).

Finally all doubts and questions seemed to be resolved, and assurance flooded in like a great tidal wave with Genesis 18:14: *"Is **anything** too hard for the Lord?"* being answered by Jeremiah 32:17: *"Ah Lord God! Behold, Thou hast made the heaven and the earth by Thy great power and stretched out arm, and there is **nothing** too hard for Thee!"*

Having questioned the Lord and received my answers, I was satisfied. But I found in my reading that the Lord had one questioning thought for me to answer:

His declaration: *"But without thy mind would I do nothing;*

that thy benefit should not be as it were of necessity, but willingly."
—Philemon 14 (KJV).

My answer: *"I delight to do Thy will, O my God."*—Psa.
40:8a (KJV).

During those days of searching following the Lord's call
to me, I shared all that I learned with John. He, too, had been
seeking the Lord's will, but hadn't felt that he had received a
personal call to serve in Micronesia as a missionary. Within
days that call came!

·   ·   ·

The following year at our Commissioning Service, John
gave this testimony of his conversion and his call:

"My life began in 1927 in New Haven, Connecticut, the
only child of Canadian parents. My early years were spent in
a liberal church. One incident stands out so clearly: the day I
asked the minister why Christ died on the cross. With the
discernment that God gives to all children, I still remember
how the big words and his hesitation shocked me into the
realization that he didn't know!

"It was not until our family was invited to visit a small
church near our vacation resort that I heard the gospel. I can
still remember the thrill of hearing for the first time the simple
good news that Christ died FOR ME. This was the beginning
of my salvation. I became convicted and ashamed, but because of the circumstances and social pressure at the time, I
didn't make a personal decision.

"In 1943 while at a youth conference at Providence, Rhode
Island, God dealt with me sternly. I was then the President of
our Youth Fellowship. Others looked to me for leadership.
Yet when the evangelist that evening called for personal workers from among the youth, all the young people in our fellowship who were present with me went forward to help and
I alone was left!

"I could not go forward and introduce others to Christ. I
suddenly realized that I didn't know Him myself. Oh, I knew

about Christ, but I had never opened my heart and committed myself fully to Him. The Lord had me on the spot. I had a head knowledge without a heart knowledge. That night Christ became my personal Savior, my sins were forgiven, and I became a new creature in Him.

". . . The first time the Lord said, 'Go,' I missed the call, confusing it with an intensified command to get others to 'pray, give and go.' But . . . the Lord not only called me audibly but visibly.

"It was a missionary conference. I had just taken my seat when my attention was called to a banner on the wall. And there it was: God's Word, which I had read and heard sung many times before, this time spelled out in two-foot-high letters. I couldn't miss it. God's spotlight was on me and the words—'So send I YOU'—were burning their message into my heart.

"There were so many difficulties: our age being past the usual maximum for missionaries, our school age children, and a recent heart condition. If there was an evangelical board with work in Micronesia, how could we be accepted? Yet the Lord had said, '*I have set before thee an open door, and no man can shut it.*'—Rev. 3:8a (KJV)."

·   ·   ·

Having the certainty of God's clear call to each of us, we rejoiced together in the assurance of Psalm 138:8 [3] and Philippians 1:6.[4] With all the promises behind us, we felt that surely the Lord would take us all the way through the wilderness, over the mountains and across the rivers to our "Promised Land"—Micronesia! We went about our work singing "The Lord Knows the Way Through the Wilderness" and "Got Any Rivers You Think Are Uncrossable?"

The Lord took us across the first great river the next day!

---

[3] "*The Lord will perfect that which concerneth me: Thy mercy, O Lord, endureth for ever: forsake not the works of Thine own hands.*" (KJV)
[4] "*Being confident of this very thing, that He which hath begun a good work in you will perform it until the day of Jesus Christ.*" (KJV)

Now that we knew we were called to Micronesia, we wondered how we could get there. Should we save our money, ask our friends to support us, and go as independent missionaries? As we prayed about it we became aware that this was not God's design for us.

We had heard of a mission board that had work in Micronesia. But what can you do with only a name—especially a name like "Liebenzell Mission"! We knew it sounded German, but that's all we knew. However, the Lord had said very clearly, *"I know thy works: behold, I have set before thee an open door, and no man can shut it: for thou hast a little strength, and hast kept My word, and hast not denied My name."*—Rev. 3:8.

There was a door open someplace. All we had to do was find it.

That day a friend of ours was traveling west. He was making a trip across country from the church which he pastored in Massachusetts. Stopping by our parsonage in Indiana, he spent a couple of hours with us. As yet we had told no one of our call. Feeling that we should take him into our confidence, we explained briefly our interest in Micronesia.

"Have you ever heard of the Liebenzell Mission?" John asked him.

"Well, yes," Bob answered slowly, "but I don't know much about it. I think their headquarters is in Germany and they have work in Micronesia."

"Do you know whether Liebenzell Mission is evangelical? That's very important to us," John explained.

"I believe it is, from what I hear," Bob responded.

"That's great," I said, joining the conversation. "But how can we contact them?"

"That's what we want to know," John added excitedly. "Could you give us an address in Germany where we might contact the Mission?"

"Oh, I'm sorry. I wouldn't have any idea what their address in Germany is," said Bob, and we wilted with disappointment.

After a few minutes of silence, John had a new idea. "I don't suppose there could be an office of the Mission here in the States, Bob?"

"Wait a minute," he answered thoughtfully. "I just remembered something! Let me tell you what happened."

We leaned forward, all ears, to hear his story. "A while back I was traveling through New Jersey, and I got lost. Finally I came to this winding road going up a small mountain. I remember, while driving up along the top of that mountain, suddenly catching sight of a little yellow sign that read 'Liebenzell Mission.' I could see that there was a lane leading back through the trees to a big resort-type house."

"Are you sure?" I exclaimed. "You really saw that in New Jersey? But where was that place?"

Breathlessly we hung on the silence, waiting for the next words. Suddenly brightening, he exclaimed, "I know right where it was! I remember seeing a little general store across the road that had a sign on it: 'Schooley's Mountain General Store.' That's where it was—on Schooley's Mountain!"

"Really?" I burst in in disbelief. "You mean the address would be Liebenzell Mission, Schooley's Mountain, New Jersey? How strange!"

"I never heard of any place like that back East," mused John.

"Why don't you give it a try?" urged Bob.

That's how the Lord led us to the Liebenzell Mission. "For God, through ways we have not known, will lead His own."[5] Hadn't the Lord promised in Isaiah 43:19 (KJV): *"Behold, I will do a new thing; now it shall spring forth; shall ye not know it? I will even make a way in the wilderness, and rivers in the desert."*

When we received an answer to our letter of inquiry, we found that the Lord had once again done *"exceeding abundantly above all that we could ask or think."*—Eph. 3:20 (KJV). As I wrote later to my father: "We asked for an evangelical board to appear out of nowhere, so to speak. God turned us to a board not only evangelical and interdenominational, but deeply

---

[5] Mrs. Charles Cowman, *Streams in the Desert*, p. 304.

spiritual as well!"

The Liebenzell Mission, it turned out, was an interdenominational faith mission with work in Germany and the Far East. It had its beginning under the inspiration of Hudson Taylor. As the Lord led that great man of God and pioneer of faith missions to develop the China Inland Mission, he was searching Europe for those who would be willing to serve in China. On a trip to Germany he came in contact with Heinrich Coerper, who was much influenced by Taylor's life and faith. So the Liebenzell Mission, which was begun by Coerper in 1899, had originally been a branch of the China Inland Mission; its first missionaries had been sent to serve in China.

Hudson Taylor's heart was big enough to feel a responsibility and burden for the tiny Micronesian Islands as well. Passing through the islands on his way to China, he wrote: "Oh, what a work for a missionary! Island after island, many almost unknown; some densely peopled, but no light, no Jesus, no hope. Can it be that Christian men and women will stay comfortably at home and leave these souls to perish? Can it be that faith has no longer the power to constrain and to sacrifice for His sake who gave His life for the world's redemption?

"Shall we think ourselves free from the responsibility to obey the plain command, 'Go ye into all the world and preach the gospel to every creature?' Is the word of our Savior no longer true, 'As My Father hath sent Me, even so send I you'? Oh, that I had a thousand tongues to proclaim in every land the riches of God's grace! Lord, raise up laborers, and thrust them forth into the harvest!"[6]

In 1906 the Father used the Liebenzell Mission to help answer Taylor's prayer. After the Mission had become independent, work was begun in Micronesia, as well as in Papua New Guinea, Taiwan and Japan.

In 1939 Henry and Anna Zimmerman had come to the United States on their way back to China to continue their missionary work. Arriving as aliens in New York with only

---

[6] J. Hudson Taylor on his voyage to China, 1854.

eight dollars, they were totally dependent on the Lord. Their "short stay" turned out to be a lengthy ministry at Schooley's Mountain, as the doors to both China and Germany were closed by World War II. The Lord laid a burden on their hearts to establish a refuge for German Liebenzell missionaries who were now displaced persons because of the war. The story of how the Lord provided 150 acres, which included the Mission farm with four large houses, is reminiscent of tales of Hudson Taylor and George Müller. This refuge for missionaries eventually developed into the U.S. headquarters for Liebenzell Mission.

Our hearts and eyes overflowed as we read stories of courage and faith in the lives of our German brethren as portrayed in Anna Zimmerman's book entitled *60 Years, Liebenzell Mission*.[7] We thrilled once again at this further evidence of the *"Lord's doing."* It was indeed *"marvelous in our eyes."*—Psa. 118:23 (KJV).

In a letter to my father dated January 11, 1962, in which I explained about our call and the Liebenzell Mission, I wrote: "It is our burning desire to be in the one place in all the world that the Lord wants us to be, and doing the particular job that He has for us to do. We cannot and must not settle for anything less than this!"

We were not, however, aware that we still had *"need of patience."*—Heb. 10:36 (KJV). The next few months we were to receive our schooling in that virtue by the Master Teacher.

---

[7] Published in West Germany by the Liebenzeller Mission (German branch of Liebenzell Mission International).

5

LEARNING PATIENCE THE HARD WAY

"Did I not tell you that if you believed, you would see the glory of God?"—John 11:40

*I*n December I found out one of the reasons why the Lord had given me such absolute assurance of my call to Micronesia. We went to visit a church in a nearby town where a pastor friend was preaching. I seldom miss any part of a sermon, because I love the Word and enjoy hearing it preached. However, that night in the little Center Church, I missed the *whole* sermon! Cal stood to read the passage of Scripture on which his thoughts were based and I heard a message especially for me—as though direct from the lips of the Lord.

"And now, behold, I go bound in the spirit unto Jerusalem, not knowing the things that shall befall me there: save that the Holy Ghost witnesseth in every city, saying that bonds and afflictions abide me. But none of these things move me, neither count I my life dear unto myself, so that I might finish my course with joy, and the ministry, which I have received of the Lord Jesus, to testify the gospel of the grace of God. And now, behold, I know that ye all, among whom I have gone preaching the kingdom of God, shall see my face no more."—Acts 20:22–25 (KJV).

I swallowed the lump that had formed in my throat and forced back the tears that were welling up within. I must not let John, who was sitting beside me, catch on to what was happening! Did the Lord really mean what He said? Would those in the United States among whom John had gone preaching as pastor and evangelist never see his face again? Yes . . .

I knew in my heart that John would go to Micronesia as the Lord had promised, but that he would never return. [1]

After the first shock of this news, I remembered the description of John in Hebrews 11:12 : *"as good **as dead.**"* In love, the Lord had chosen to give him a few extra years in which to lead islanders to Christ. I didn't know how many years would be wrapped up in that gift, but since one term with the Liebenzell Mission was six years, I judged that it would be fewer than that. Yet the promise had been for *much fruit*!

I knew that the Lord was waiting for me to submit to His decision. It was painful! But finally I was able to say, "Your will be done. I have no right to cling to John who is Your man following Your agenda. You must choose for him and for me. I leave his future and mine in Your loving hands."

As I digested this unusual revelation over the next few days, I wondered whether to share it or not. Should I tell John? Would the information help him to use the few years left to their fullest? Or would it be a dark shadow hanging over his head, hindering him from doing his best work? I couldn't answer these questions. I just didn't know.

I finally reconciled my dilemma by praying, "Lord, if You want John or anyone else to know, You will have to tell them. I can't take the responsibility for what the knowledge might do to others. I will tell no one until John is gone." Then I thanked Him for this unusual look into the future, recognizing that it was God's loving way of preparing me ahead of time for *"the valley of the shadow of death"* (Psa. 23:4, KJV) through which I would pass.[2]

The lesson in patience had only begun. On January first, I was reading for my devotions from the book of Exodus. I was thinking about the way the children of Israel moved through the wilderness, as described in Exodus 40:36–37.[3] Being interested in God's guidance through the cloud, I turned

---

[1] See principle #4, Appendix.

[2] See principle #5, Appendix.

[3] *"And when the cloud was taken up from over the tabernacle, the children of Israel went onward in all their journeys: but if the cloud were not taken up, then they journeyed not till the day that it was taken up."* (KJV)

to the marginal reference in Numbers 10:11. There I found another unusual message. It said that the cloud was taken up on the twentieth day of the second month, and then the Israelites began to move. The message to me was: Something is going to happen on the twentieth day of the second month.

In an attempt to reason out what this might mean, I thought of our impatient waiting for word from the Liebenzell Mission, to which we had applied, as a cloud that must be removed. I decided that on February 20th we would receive the word we were awaiting and begin our journey to our "Promised Land."

I was wrong!

On February 20th John was in the Veterans' Hospital and I was driving with breaking heart down to Indianapolis to see him. Alone in the car with only the Lord as my companion for the fifty miles, I quizzed Him accusingly, "Why did this happen? You could have prevented this heart attack, Lord. Now what will become of our missionary calling? After all, we didn't dream this all up. You called us and gave us all those promises. Now what? It's more impossible than ever! Why???"

With empty heart, I tried to encourage John and give him a confidence in the future that I didn't feel. I didn't mention our missionary call. He was in the intensive care unit, and I knew that I mustn't give him the slightest indication of my troubled thoughts.

That evening back home, weary and heartsick, I reached for my Bible and turned to the book of Numbers where I had been reading. Coming to the 19th verse of chapter 23, I read, *"God is not a man, that He should lie; neither the son of man, that He should repent: hath He said, and shall He not do it? Or hath He spoken, and shall He not make it good?"*

Falling to my knees before the Almighty God of heaven and earth, I wept, "O Lord, please forgive me! How could I ever question Your judgments? You're not a man like we are. When You say something, You do it. You keep every promise You make. Forgive me for doubting You. I know that You will do all that You have said."

Reading on through verse 24, I found what seemed to be a special message, but I didn't understand it. So I took our call to the field—all the promises God had given regarding it (including that one about the 20th day of the second month)—and added to them this strange message. I wrapped them all together in a mental package, tied it securely, and passed it to the Lord with these words, "This is Your responsibility. Since I cannot understand it, I leave it with You. I'm through worrying. I believe that someday I'll see You fulfill all Your promises—though how You'll do it, I can't imagine." [4]

Then I turned to the problems at hand. The church had been growing steadily. Souls were being saved and Christians edified. We had several weekly services and four active youth groups. With John in the hospital, the whole work could well suffer a crippling blow. I simply could not stand by and let it happen.

Reminding the Lord of what He already knew, I prayed, "Here I am, useless, worthless—nothing! I have neither the time nor the wisdom to prepare messages for all these meetings and organizations. But, Lord, You know there is a hungry congregation waiting and I am responsible somehow to do what I can. I cannot feed them, but You can. I offer myself to You. You must give me the thoughts and words."

The following day the congregation was a bit stunned as I offered myself to be their interim pastor until John should recover. Perhaps they were even more surprised as the Holy Spirit strangely moved their hearts through the message the Lord had given me at midnight the night before. It was obvious that it was *"not I, but Christ"* (Gal. 2:20, KJV) who spoke.

Thus began a period of several weeks in which I walked again on that miraculous sea. All day long, through each successive day of housework, cooking, sermon preparation, care of the children, traveling the hundred-mile round trip to the hospital, planning and preaching, my heart sang! The Lord was there every moment by my side, at my elbow, leaning

---

[4] See principle #6, Appendix.

over my shoulder—guiding my thoughts and whispering sweet messages of comfort and assurance. I cried with David from the depths of my being, *"How great is Your goodness . . ."* —Psa. 31:19–24.

When John began to improve a little, we finally had the courage to talk together about our call. I showed him the verses of assurance the Lord had given, and together we rejoiced in the knowledge that somehow He would find the way to fulfill all that He had promised. Someday we would serve Him in Micronesia.

"But, hon, why do you think the Lord let this happen?" questioned John. "What do you think is the purpose of it all?"

"I really don't know, dear, but one of the things the Lord has shown me is that *'God led the people around by the desert road.'*[5] I assume that was because they weren't ready yet!"

Then, opening my Bible to Hebrews 10:36, I said, "This morning the reading in *Streams in the Desert* used this verse. It really made me stop and think about myself. Listen. *'For ye have need of patience, that, after ye have done the will of God, ye might receive the promise.'* To be honest, I think I was too impatient. Maybe I thought I knew everything about the will of God, and didn't recognize, until this happened, that I still have lots to learn."

After sitting a few moments in thoughtful silence, John spoke softly. "Oh, you're so right, dear. There's still so much I, too, need to learn of patience and pleasing the Lord. Isn't He wonderful? He knows just what we need!"

But the Lord chose to continue the lesson on patience much longer than we had thought necessary . . .

I wrote to my father on March 19, 1962:

Well, we have our best half home with us again! Last Friday, after four weeks in the hospital, Jack [John's nickname] was released to come home. . . . Everyone seemed to think that I should be so relieved not to have to drive that 100 miles every day any more. But I really didn't even think of it as difficult. The Lord gave grace and

---

[5] Exodus 13:18.

strength for that as for everything. I must repeatedly thank Him for His tender, loving care of me during this time. I never had the first bit of trouble with the car, though it is in pretty bad shape and needs several things. . . . God answered my prayers in so many cases before I could even ask. I know it was because so many people were praying.

The doctors said that when Jack was released he could take up his work little by little as he regains his strength. In a month he should be able to carry the full load. Jack went to church yesterday against my better judgment. But it didn't seem to hurt him at all. He took it very slowly. I conducted the service and gave the message: "Why Was I Born?"—regarding the unanswered questions of our teenagers and about wasted lives with no real purpose. We looked for the answers in one of the oldest books in the Bible—Job.

At the close of the service, eleven young people from 13 to 20 came forward in answer to the call: "Whom shall I send? And who will go for Us?" They answered, "Here we are, Lord. Send us!" How we praise God for the way He is working in the lives of our young people.

We have not heard anything definite yet from Liebenzell. We have left it all in the Lord's hands. He knows that we are willing to go or stay, and to do whatever He wants as long as we have the privilege of serving Him. This close brush with death in no way changes the picture, as far as we are concerned, unless to make us more conscious than ever of the necessity of using the time we have together to its fullest for the Lord's glory.

We had expected John to make rapid improvement, but he didn't. After several weeks had passed, one morning we read together, *"My brethren, count it all joy when ye fall into divers temptations; knowing this, that the trying of your faith worketh patience. But let patience have her perfect work, that ye may be perfect and entire, wanting nothing."*—James 1:2–4 (KJV).

Looking into each other's eyes, we smiled. Our faith was

being tried because we needed patience. But in our impatience to learn our lesson of patience, we had forgotten that the Lord is never in a hurry. With Him *"one day is . . . as a thousand years, and a thousand years as one day."*—2 Peter 3:8 (KJV). He wanted us to have time to perfect our patience by waiting on Him.

By the middle of May, John had made only slight improvement. He would be exhausted after preaching one message. He never slept all night. Because of the pains in his chest he would get up and sit, sometimes for hours, in a chair. He was taking several kinds of medicine, including a blood thinner. Nitroglycerine alone could bring temporary relief.

One day I turned once again to the verses in Numbers 23 which I had read when John was in the hospital. The Lord had promised to bless and He would (vss. 20, 21, & 23a). Some day we would look back to this time and say, *"What hath God wrought!"* (vs. 23b). In amazement, I saw that the promise for John was that he would have *"the strength of a unicorn"* and would *"lift up himself as a young lion"* (vss. 22 & 24)! From the end of verse 24, I realized that he would *"not lie down"* in death until he had finished the work to which he had been called.

I was puzzled by the first part of verse 24: *"Behold, the people shall rise up as a great lion."* Suddenly it struck! Running out to the living room, I found John sitting in an easy chair, deep in thought.

I startled him with my sudden exclamation. "We believe the Lord can heal. Right?"

"Well, of course. We've seen Him do it many times. But what are you getting at, dear?" John asked, puzzled.

"You and I have been praying that the Lord would heal you, but He hasn't. Just now it hit me that maybe He wants us to ask the *people* to pray!"

Still perplexed, John asked, "What do you mean? Our people have been praying for me since February."

"Yes, I know," I hurried on, impatient to get my idea across. "But we never thought of having them come together in one place to pray specifically for your immediate healing!"

"That's true! Do you think that's what we should do?"

"Yes, hon, and I think we should do it right away."

The next day as we typed out the bulletin to be mimeo-graphed we added at the bottom these words, "All those who would like to pray specifically for the healing of the pastor are invited to stay after the regular evening service. Please don't stay unless you believe God will answer!"

Sunday arrived. As I sat in church waiting for the morning service to begin, my mind turned back five months to the first of January. I had not thought about that strange message in Numbers 10:11[6] for some time. All at once it dawned on me that the Jewish calendar is used in the Bible, not our calendar. I leafed quickly through my Bible to an Old Testament reference to the first month. In the margin was the word "April." If the first month was April, then the second month must have been May. With trembling fingers I opened the bulletin to check the date. There it was at the top: "Sunday, May 20, 1962." There I sat on *"the twentieth day of the second (Jewish) month!"*

And that evening *"the cloud"* moved just as the faithful Lord had promised. That hovering black cloud of pain and helplessness which had kept us under its shadow for so many months was swept away by the Almighty's hand as the people knelt around the altar of our church and cried out to Him in faith.[7]

In a letter to my father dated May 23, 1962, I wrote:

Praise the Lord! Great is His faithfulness! God has answered prayer and Jack is healed! . . . As you said, Daddy, we have not seen the complete fulfillment of God's promises yet, but we know that we have them. Hold on in prayer with us until we see it all. God bless you for your faith!

We had a big crowd at Sunday evening service and most of them stayed on till the 9 o'clock prayer meeting.

---

[6] *"And it came to pass on the twentieth day of the second month . . . that the cloud was taken up . . ."* (KJV)

[7] See principle #7, Appendix.

Before we prayed, I read 1 John 5:14–15[8] and explained that many people stumble over the phrase *"according to His will."* I wanted them to know that we felt sure that this was according to God's will, because the Lord gave me these promises from Numbers 23 while Jack was still in the hospital: *"He hath as it were the strength of an unicorn* (a two-horned wild bull)."—Num. 23:22b (KJV). *"Behold, the people shall rise up as a great lion, and he shall lift himself up as a young lion: he shall not lie down until he eat of the prey, and drink the blood of the slain"*; in other words, "until he tastes the spoils of victory that God has for him."—Num. 23:24 (KJV).

Not fully understanding them, I have mulled over these verses for three months—believing them, but not knowing how God would work them out. I thought maybe Jack would just gradually get better, like the doctors said he would. But verse 23b didn't fit into that at all: *"According to this time it shall be said . . . What hath God wrought!"*

To go back to Sunday night: Next we read Mark 11:22–24,[9] and I explained that we didn't want anyone to come forward to pray unless they could pray in faith *"and doubt not in their hearts."* Then we turned to James 5:14–16.[10] I asked them to pray silently, confessing their own sins first; then gave an opportunity for public confession. Then we called them down to the altar. I think about everyone

---

[8] "This is the confidence that we have in approaching God: that if we ask anything according to His will, He hears us. And if we know that He hears us—whatever we ask—we know that we have what we asked of Him."

[9] "'Have faith in God,' Jesus answered. 'I tell you the truth, if anyone says to this mountain, "Go, throw yourself into the sea," and does not doubt in his heart but believes that what he says will happen, it will be done for him. Therefore I tell you, whatever you ask for in prayer, believe that you have received it, and it will be yours.'"

[10] "Is any one of you sick? He should call the elders of the church to pray over him and anoint him with oil in the name of the Lord. And the prayer offered in faith will make the sick person well; the Lord will raise him up. If he has sinned, he will be forgiven. Therefore confess your sins to each other so that you may be healed. The prayer of a righteous man is powerful and effective."

WALKING THE WAVES

prayed—brief, but prayers of faith. We've never seen a prayer meeting quite like it.

We have been traveling through a dark tunnel for so long, with the exception of the light coming from above when we looked up in faith. It hardly seems possible that we are now nearing the end of the tunnel, with the sunlight getting brighter every moment.

6

Even the Children, Lord?

"If you're ever going to do anything, do it NOW!" [1]

*T*he Lord's clock runs with split-second timing. May 20th had arrived. The dark cloud was swept away. It was time to move to the field. But all those months we had waited in vain for an answer from the Liebenzell Mission. On May 24th, there it was in our post office box! With great excitement we tore open the envelope. "You have been accepted for work with the Liebenzell Mission on the Palau Islands."

Having danced around the room a few times, we sat down, breathless, to consider the magnificent work of our great God. Had we received our answer from the Mission before this very week, we would have had to write back saying that we could not go because of John's health. Now he was strong again, able to accept the call and do the work.

Finally we went back to reading the letter. It went on to say that our acceptance was conditional. Our children seemed to be the unsolved problem. At that time, Sandy, our son, was nine and Angela was six. The Mission wanted to assign us primarily as teachers at the Bethania Girls' High School in Palau. They needed both of us to teach full-time.

The problem was outlined in the letter:

> In Ngaraard, on one of the Palau Islands, where the Girls' School is located, there is no school for American children. If one of you has to teach the children by correspondence, this one would hardly have time for any mis-

---

[1] Bob Pierce, World Vision.

sion work or for learning the language. Usually missionary children have to be left in the homeland for their education when about 12 years of age, or even earlier. Sorry, we do not have a missionary children's home here.

Would you know a way to solve this problem? Would you be willing to be separated from your children for the Lord's sake? Would there be a possibility that relatives or friends would give your children a home in order to get the proper education? There is an American school in Guam which would be nearer to the islands, but this is not a boarding school. We would have to find a Christian home for the children there.

The monthly allowances our missionaries receive for their personal needs are $75.00 per person and $18.00 for each child, as the Lord provides. We have experienced that the Lord is faithful, and He will not fail you.

Leaving our beautiful homeland, facing years of separation from relatives and friends, selling our furniture and car, giving up the security of a good-paying pastorate—all of these "sacrifices" had been carefully considered and dismissed. Now they seemed like only a drop in the bucket compared to the magnitude of the decision before us.

John's reaction was immediate and explosive. "That's impossible! We just won't do it. Let's write what we think about this idea!"

"Now, just a minute, dear. Let's not be hasty. I think we should give it a few days of prayer and consideration before we return our answer to them. I don't like the idea any more than you do, but I think we should be careful first to find out what the Lord thinks about it."

"Yes, you're right, of course," John concurred with a sigh. "But, honestly, hon, I think this is asking too much."

"I thought so, too, when the Lord first started to talk to me about the children." Then I went on to relate to him the experience that I had had a few weeks before.

I had been thinking a great deal about Abraham again. John had been sick so long with so little improvement that I felt almost ready to give up hope. Then I read once again about that great man of faith in Romans 4:18 (KJV): *"Who against hope believed in hope, that he might become the father of nations, according to that which was spoken, 'So shall thy seed be!'"*

It had been such an encouragement to me to recall the fact that Abraham had nothing in which to hope except God's word to him. That day, as I read on in the book of Romans, the God of Abraham had given *me* His word of hope: *"And the God of peace shall bruise Satan under your feet shortly."*—Rom. 16:20 (KJV). What a thrill it was to look back now to see the way this promise, too, had been fulfilled!

All day that day, as I had gone about doing the housework, my mind had been on that mighty patriarch. Through my head went humming the refrain, "Give me a faith like his." In the midst of the ironing, the Lord suddenly "painted out" for me the faith of Abraham in a new light. I saw the picture of the obedient Abraham, knife in hand, climbing Mount Moriah with Isaac at his side. [2]

Then came the questions: "What would you have done? Do you have the faith of Abraham? What will you do when I ask *your* son?"

Leaving the ironing board already wet with tears, I stumbled into the bedroom and closed the door. I must be alone with the Lord to face this greatest of all tests. I didn't need to open my Bible because I knew well the verses in Luke 14. Now they came pouring into my mind: *"If any man come to Me, and hate not his father, and mother, and wife, and children, and brethren, and sisters, yea, and his own life also, he cannot be My disciple. . . . Likewise, whosoever he be of you that forsaketh not all that he hath, he cannot be My disciple."*—Luke 14:26, 33 (KJV). [3]

A lengthy time of weeping and soul-searching passed before I was able to place my darling Angela and my precious Sandy forever in the Lord's hands. It had seemed that they already belonged to Him. After all, we had given them

---

[2] The story of the sacrificial offering of Isaac by Abraham in Genesis 22:1–18.

[3] See principle #8, Appendix.

to Him before birth, and dedicated them to Him at a few months of age. Each had already made his/her own decision to give his/her heart to Christ. But all of this had been somehow in the realm of the complacent Christian home. Now I had stepped off solid ground onto those sometimes turbulent waves, and the Lord was asking me to put my two sweet children out onto the same water.

Having faced with all honesty the possible eventualities ahead, I was finally able to say, "Whether it means separation, disability, or even death, Lord, they are Yours. I trust You, even with my most precious of all possessions, my children."

The Lord gave me a promise that day about the children which, in later years, became the life preserver thrown to the bereaved, whose feet had begun to sink in the icy waves of disappointment and despair. *"And all thy children shall be taught of the Lord; and great shall be the peace of thy children."*—Isa. 54:13 (KJV).

Rising from my knees, I felt as though I had fought a great battle. Exhausted, I sank into a chair and thought again of Abraham. I had gained a new respect for him. I was beginning to see what it had cost him to have such a mighty faith. Turning once again to Hebrews 11, I read that brief summary of his life. Coming to verses 17 through 19,[4] I discovered a new thought. Although Abraham had given Isaac wholly to the Lord, even to death, he had *"received him"* again as if from the dead. "Perhaps the Lord will do the same for me," I thought, never guessing the accuracy of that prophecy. "Anyway, I won't be afraid to trust Him for whatever may come. He knows best!"

John had been silent as I related this moving experience. Though his head was bowed on his chest, I could see the teardrops falling, leaving small wet spots on the legs of his trousers. I knew that within was raging that most difficult of all

[4] *"By faith Abraham, when he was tried, offered up Isaac: and he that had received the promises offered up his only begotten son, of whom it was said, 'That in Isaac shall thy seed be called': accounting that God was able to raise him up, even from the dead; from whence also he received him in figure."* (KJV)

battles. Finally, clearing his throat and lifting his head, he spoke, "It's not an easy road, is it, dear?" Kneeling together, with arms about each other, we committed Sandy and Angela forever to the Lord.

The next day we discussed again the letter we must write to the Mission.

"Honestly, I don't know what we should say," John fretted. "I know the Lord does not want us to leave our children here at home with someone. I also don't feel that it would be best for them to be in Guam, even though I'm willing to have them wherever the Lord wants them."

"Well, I don't think they should be in Guam either. I really feel that they should be with us at least for a few years. But we've committed them to the Lord, so let's leave the decision with Him," I suggested.

"But how can we do that?"

"Let's write to the Mission that we are willing for them to stay in Guam if the Lord works it out that way. We know we can trust Him to work it out for the best," I finished confidently.

John wrote our answer to the Mission:

We have thought and prayed much about the problem of our children's education. The Lord has given us the privilege and responsibility of raising our children. It is our greatest desire that our children be raised and trained spiritually so they might be fitted for the Lord's service in later life. For this reason we do not feel they should be entrusted to the care of relatives.

Do you feel that there may be a good possibility of finding a Christian home for them on Guam? Do you have any in mind? Would it be permissible for the children to be with us during their school vacation? We are depending on the Lord to work out arrangements for our children that are pleasing to Him.

During the following month, as we waited for a response to our letter, we tried to prepare the children for whatever answer might come, meanwhile hoping that we, too, would be prepared when the time came. During those days my thoughts and prayers were centered almost entirely on the children. I realized that the present circumstance was only the first of a long series of decisions which would have to be made through the years ahead.

One day I decided to take the Lord at His word: *"Ask of Me things to come concerning My sons."*—Isa. 45:11b (KJV). I asked about things to come for Sandy and Angela. The answer came in Isaiah 60:4b (KJV): *"Thy sons shall come from far, and thy daughters shall be nursed at thy side."* I thanked the Lord for this insight into the future, and then tucked it away in the cupboards of my mind with that other prophecy concerning John's death and the many promises about the future of all Micronesia.

When the answer came from the Mission, it was proven once again that we need not fear the Lord's will. It is always safe to trust His perfect wisdom. It seemed that the missionary couple in Guam, whom the Mission leaders had contacted, would be unable to keep our children in their home. The only alternative was that we take them with us, at least temporarily.

The senior missionary at the Bethania High School had written also, advising the leaders to have us bring our children. This would mean that I would teach them mornings and teach in the high school in the afternoons. On weekends we would be doing evangelistic work in the neighboring villages on Babeldaob,[5] the largest island, and during school vacations reaching other islands in the Palau group. We were asked if this was agreeable. Laughing a bit hysterically over such an unnecessary question, we quickly penned our agreement.

"This seems like a job too difficult for us," I wrote to my father. "But the Lord continually reassures us in His Word: *'Faithful is He that calleth you, who also will do it.'*—1 Thess. 5:24 (KJV). How can we back out on the Lord after He has opened

---

[5] Spelled "Babelthuap" on some older maps.

every door in His perfect time, and made the crooked places straight?"

So it was on the first day of September that I began the most challenging work I had ever tackled—teaching my own children in the midst of change and turmoil. We had had a yard sale in the backyard of the parsonage, at which we sold or gave away about ninety percent of our belongings. We had said tearful good-byes to all our dear friends in Indiana. Pulling a small trailer loaded with John's desk and filing cabinet, plus household linens and dishes, we headed for the Mission headquarters in New Jersey. There, on August 17, 1962, we were commissioned to serve the Lord under the Liebenzell Mission.

To our friends and supporters John wrote:

When we arrived here things were already buzzing on the grounds, with guests arriving for the big, annual Missionary Day. And what a day it was! Special music, singing, Christian fellowship and special German cooking like we've never tasted in our lives.

The highlight of the day was the afternoon service. There must have been 400 people present. The music was out of this world! There was a men's a cappella choir and a German brass band. At 4:30 P.M. Juanita and I and another couple were commissioned as missionaries—they to the island of Manus and we to the Palau Islands. After we gave our testimonies, the leaders of the Mission admonished us, laid their hands upon us and prayed. The Holy Spirit was present in great power. The admonitions from old German missionaries who had served the Lord in China many years ago broke our hearts again.

We were ready to go to the field, but the necessary entry permits had not yet arrived, so we had to wait. While waiting, I began teaching Sandy fifth grade and Angela second grade, using the Calvert Course. I learned very quickly that the one ingredient essential to the teaching of one's own children is DISCIPLINE! I found that I must discipline myself first—a most challenging task. Next, I must be able to discipline the children without killing their incentive to learn. Last, and definitely not least, I must discipline all of those around us who felt impelled to interrupt our progress!

I didn't realize at the time that the task would grow increasingly difficult through the six years of homeschooling which were to follow. On the field, people did not understand that I had only the morning hours in which to teach my children, and we were constantly interrupted. I could politely ask the school staff to leave us alone during the mornings, but when our Palauan brothers and sisters came, it would have been very rude if I had mentioned such a thing or even indicated impatience. When we fell behind in our school days, sometimes we ended up doing lessons in the bottom of our diesel boat on the way to another village or island. We couldn't do that for long, however, before one or the other of the children started turning green!

When I struggled with discouragement over our unyielding time schedule and incessant interruptions, I would often experience a sense of failure and fear. I was sure that I was single-handedly ruining my children. They would probably never amount to anything with this kind of schooling! It was then that the Lord comforted me with that brief verse: *"Have faith in God!"*—Mark 11:22. On one of those occasions I read, "Have faith that He knows all, sympathizes with all, can rectify what is amiss in all!"[6] From then on, my prayer was "Lord, please rectify what is amiss!"

Yet, were I to live those years over, I would beg once again to have my children at my side. It was well worth it all!

Another formidable mountain came into view during those weeks at the Mission headquarters. Because the students at Bethania High School came from various areas of Micronesia—their native languages being Palauan, Yapese, Chuukese, Pohnpeian, Kosraean and Marshallese—the language we would use in the classroom was English. But to be

---

[6] Mrs. Charles E. Cowman, *Springs in the Valley*, p. 8.

effective missionaries among the people of Palau, a mastery of Palauan was called for. And that would not be easy.

We were fortunate to be able to spend two weeks at Schooley's Mountain with a missionary who had been in Palau. Ingelore Lengning, having served six years on the field, had achieved fluency in the Palauan language. Since it is spoken by only about 16,000 people, and only on those five small inhabited islands that make up part of the Palau chain,[7] a missionary cannot begin to learn Palauan until he arrives at his station. We were to have the privilege of learning a little of the language before departure from the States.

I used every spare minute to ply Ingelore with questions. "What's the Palauan for this? How do you say . . . ?" Not trusting my memory, I carried a small notebook around.

All the information gained I transcribed into a bigger alphabetical notebook. By the time Ingelore had to leave for Wisconsin, I had collected a fair-sized store of materials.

After "school" the children would go out to play and I would go to work on my notebook. "Now all I have to do is learn this," I thought. But, oh, the agony of trying to remember all those strange-looking words. Why, I couldn't even recall how to pronounce some of them! I'd stare at words like "nglunguuch" (prayer) and "cheldechuderreng" (wrath) and wonder if I would ever be able to say them! As John wrote to friends, "It's enough to scare the stripes off a zebra!"

Finally, my head bursting with things I could not say or understand, I exploded, "Lord, I'll never get this language! I'm just too stupid. Why did you call me to do something I can't do?"

That night, before I went to sleep, my compassionate Friend spoke peace to my troubled mind in my devotions. There it was—another promise waiting only to be claimed: *"The heart also of the rash shall understand knowledge, and the tongue of the stammerers shall be ready to speak plainly."*—Isa. 32:4 (KJV). I laughed out loud as I read that accurate descrip-

---

[7] Babeldaob, Oreor (formerly Koror), Kayangel, Beliliou (formerly Peleliu), and Ngeaur (formerly Angaur).

tion of my Palauan. I was a "stammerer" for sure!

Almost six years later, I remembered this verse as I stood on the island shore ready to embark on my first furlough to the United States. One of the dear Palauan deacons had come to say good-bye. As I looked at his weatherworn face, I reflected briefly on all that had transpired in those six eventful years since I had first met him on that same white beach. I knew he was remembering too, because his voice broke when he finally spoke.

"Will you come back to Palau?" he asked in his language.

"You know that Palau will always be my home," I spoke easily in those now familiar words. "But if the Lord should send me to other islands in Micronesia, I must go. For He continually reminds me of those islands where there are no missionaries."

"But, Mrs. Pastor, you *must* come back to Palau. You are one of the missionaries whom we can really understand. You speak so plainly!"

I smiled, recalling the promise and how literally the Lord had fulfilled it. "Yes," I thought, "plainly—not perfectly. I guess, after all, that *plainness* is all that's necessary."

Turning to the waiting deacon, I said seriously, "I must return to Micronesia, because the Lord has called me to serve Him here the rest of my life. Will you pray that He will lead me to the islands where He can use me best, whether it be my beloved Palau or some other?"

"I will not forget to pray for you" were his parting words.

7

ARRIVAL IN PARADISE

"My tomorrows are all known to Thee. Thou wilt lead me all the way." [1]

"*I* tried to call you from Idlewild [2] and didn't get any answer. I wanted to say, 'Good-bye for now. I love you very much. And God be with you.' But I guess you know all these things. Yesterday morning, at the service at Schooley's Mountain, Jack and I sang '*Follow, I Will Follow Thee.*' The chorus reads, 'My tomorrows are all known to Thee. Thou wilt lead me all the way.' How thankful I am that we are in the Lord's hands. We go in His hands and we leave you in His hands. And someday we will have eternity together to talk over all that the Lord has done for us."

My letter to my father and stepmother was written on the second leg of our long journey to our "island paradise." We had written in a prayer letter before that: "The 15th of October is 'M' day for the Simpsons. Wish you could grab your hat and coat (sunhat and raincoat!) and blast off with us. None of us has ever been aboard a jet before!"

The letter went on to describe our helicopter flight from Newark to New York, and the three jet flights over the country and across the vast Pacific. It ended with our anticipated arrival in Palau: "By evening (ten days after our arrival on Guam and flight to Palau) we should have made our way from civilization through the crystal-clear ocean and over the

---

[1] "*Follow, I Will Follow Thee,*" by Howard and Margaret Brown; copyright 1935; renewal 1963; Folio Publishing Rights assigned to Singspiration.
[2] Name of JFK Airport in New York at that time.

reefs by Mission boat to our faraway jungle island with the strange-sounding name—the very place of God's choosing and ministry for us. This is a place of palm trees and coconuts, pounding surf and every tropical beauty, but a place where men are bound by heathenism and superstition, without Christ and without eternal hope. Pray for us as we hold high the Light of Life in this dark island world."

As it turned out, the flights were all great except the last part of the leg from Honolulu to Guam. We flew through the edge of a typhoon. It was about 3:30 A.M. and the stewardesses were trying to serve breakfast before our early morning arrival in Guam. The food was bouncing off the trays, a couple of the stewardesses were thrown to the floor, and my kids were losing their last few meals!

Climbing down the steps from the plane, we were met by a wall of humidity that took our breath away and made our legs a little more wobbly. Just outside the quonset "terminal" we met the Feys, who had recently returned to the islands from Germany. Their immediate impression of us was not good. "Your children look sickly! I don't think you should be taking them to Palau."

Surprised, I looked at Sandy and Angela, and sure enough, their complexion was sallow and green-tinged. I hastened to explain that our children were quite healthy but that we had had a very rough plane trip in which the plane kept dropping sharply. They weren't convinced even when the stewardess said that it was her worst flight ever.

We spent about ten days on Guam. The card I wrote to my Dad described it. "We are really busy these days, scurrying around trying to find the things we need to take with us. They vary all the way from junk salvage to exorbitant new merchandise. The secret is to find the bargains in-between. We are depending on the Lord to help us."

My next letter was written on the *Errol*, a little freighter which plied the waters between Guam and Palau. We had expected to fly that 800 miles and had reservations to do so. Much to our consternation, we were told one day by Pastor

Fey that he had decided to cancel our flight and put us on the *Errol* instead. He thought we could take our purchases with us, but as it turned out, we couldn't take anything but our suitcases.

I wrote:

> Well, we have sighted Yap, and should be there by early evening. Imagine sailing into Yap! It sounds like a fairy tale. This whole voyage seems like something from a book I may have read once. I just saw a coconut floating, and it reminded me of Columbus and how he must have felt when he sighted land after so long at sea.
>
> This leg of our voyage is very interesting. Our "ship" is a small freighter. It is so small that it rolls all the time. The sea is calm today, but it still rolls. We have had some very hard rains and rough seas at times ("typhoon season"), but it could have been much worse.
>
> I asked the Lord to keep us all from seasickness, because I felt that it was important to our ministry. Since we will be doing a lot of ocean travel around Babeldaob, it could be a great hindrance to our work for any of us to have a fear or dread of the ocean. The Lord graciously answered my prayer and we have all been fine.
>
> This is a far cry from a luxury liner. We are in a big "cabin" with two Palauan women and three children. The bunks are sort of hammock-bunks in threes and twos. They are so close together you can't sit up in them. [I didn't tell them that underneath the thin mattresses scurried all manner of insect life.] With all the luggage in the cabin, there is just room to walk through. At the end is a small bathroom with a so-called shower. On one side of the "cabin" there is just screening and canvas, so the rain comes in when it rains hard.
>
> The deck is loaded with freight, so there is just enough room to walk around. [I didn't tell them that with all the rain, the deck was slippery and rather dangerous for the children.] The food is more or less edible. [I didn't tell them that the usual fare was fish heads and rice.] Actu-

ally, we don't mind any of it. We are thoroughly enjoying our trip and are thankful for every new experience.

The only Palauan town of any size is Koror, on a small but centralized island also called Koror. It was there that the freighter docked. We disembarked and were met by several missionaries and a bevy of singing boys from the school there. We had traveled nearly halfway around the globe.

We were then taken on the Bethania diesel boat up the eastern side of the big island (30 x 8 miles) of Babeldaob. During our five-hour journey we breathed in all the extravagant beauty of this place we now called "home."

As the boat slipped through the crystal-clear water, we gazed in amazement at the variegated corals and myriads of tropical fish below us. We expected the boat to run aground. It seemed as if we could touch the bottom if we were to hang over the boat far enough. The boatsman informed us that we were looking into fifteen feet of that aqua-colored water!

The green hills of Babeldaob were liberally sprinkled with coconut trees rising above the mangrove swamps at the shore. Five times we sighted piers extending out from small villages, while on our right there was always the pounding surf on the fringing reef. Finally we sighted a white beach with great ironwood trees at the shore. It was Ngaraard! We had arrived!

Our "paradise" was more beautiful than had been described to us, but it was not without its problems. The workers had been working on our house, but it wasn't finshed. The absence of screens allowed in even more than the usual population of flies, mosquitoes, gnats, geckoes, cockroaches, etc. Since our outside bathroom and shower had not been completed, we used the lady missionaries' "benjo" down the path a ways. We found it already occupied by rats—who were not very pleased with our presence and ran around above our heads to disconcert us as we used the facility.

The "difficulties and hardships" didn't even make an impact on me. After eighteen long years, the Lord had finally allowed me to serve Him as a missionary. I was in seventh heaven! When the schoolgirls sang, I was sure I was hearing an angelic choir. (Later, when I was their music teacher, they didn't sound quite so angelic to me.)

I wondered if the weather was always so windy and rainy. Then we heard that a major typhoon had hit Guam ten days after we left, completely demolishing the two churches where John had preached and the little cabin where we had stayed. How thankful we were to be in Palau where there was only wind and rain.

It was a bit disconcerting the day we got the news that probably all our possessions were lost! Our four drums and one crate had been at the wharf when the typhoon came barreling in, and the report was that everything at the wharf had been washed overboard. The beds, dressers, kerosene stove, sinks, etc., were still in storage when the storm hit and most of the warehouses were destroyed. The old kerosene refrigerator which we had bought had been buried under a roof, but they were "sending it anyway"!

"Well, Lord, maybe we are here for our six-year term with only our suitcases! That means that You are going to be busy finding the things we will need for living." But the Lord chose to rescue some of our belongings from Guam, and we were able to order mattresses and some other essentials from Sears' mail-order catalog. And the refrigerator worked! In fact, we used the old thing for several years.

My letters were always full of the special ways in which the Father was blessing us. It seemed that He was enjoying fulfilling His promises in Psalm 37:3–5![3] I wrote:

> The Lord has been good to send us what we need. We often don't have what many people call necessities, but there always seems to be a substitute. We are on our last can of yeast, and there is no more in Koror (the market town) and won't be until the ship comes at the end of April. So I guess we will need to substitute something for bread one of these days.

---

[3] *"Trust in the Lord and do good; dwell in the land and enjoy safe pasture. Delight yourself in the Lord and He will give you the desires of your heart. Commit your way to the Lord; trust in Him and He will do this."*

To show how generously the Lord takes care of us: I was concerned last week about the lack of vitamins in our diet. We hadn't had any fresh fruit or vegetables for a couple of weeks. Sometimes we can buy these in Koror, but a ship hasn't been in for a while, so there's nothing fresh there.

So I prayed about it. The next two days we received the following from people as gifts: two pineapples, half of a small watermelon, a bunch of bananas, a small basket of green, sour fruit, a big white fruit (a little like a pear inside), a big bunch of kangkum (a green, leafy vegetable, a little like beet greens), four cucumbers, and enough green beans for two meals. Isn't the Lord wonderful!

The blessings coming down from the Lord's hands were not just material gifts. Before we had left home we had asked people to apply Paul's prayer request to us: *"Devote yourselves to prayer, being watchful and thankful. And pray for us, that God may open a door for our message, so that we may proclaim the mystery of Christ. . . ."*—Col. 4:2–3. Many must have been asking the Lord for this because we were seeing His answers!

In January 1963, John wrote to supporters and friends:

The Lord's presence and blessing is abundant here. When I gave the invitation this morning, many raised their hands for prayer. Two, a young Palauan father and a girl, found their way, in tears, to the foot of the cross. Two more names were written in the Lamb's Book of Life because you prayed. Two more to work as His disciples because you have been faithful to stand with us, your missionaries.

Oh, how I wish that you could just once stand with me in the preaching services and see their faces as the message of the cross is unfolded through the interpreter. Believe us when we say that these pleasant victories are wrought by prayer and fasting. We are pleased to report thirty others, like the two mentioned above, who have come to a personal saving knowledge of Christ in the last two months. This is a cause for double rejoicing because all of our ministering has to be done through an interpreter.

If we have a main prayer request it is this: *Pray that we will learn the language!* . . . It's the hardest thing we have ever done, but God's strength is great. Are you ready for your Palauan lesson for today? The word is "kngtmam" (our sin). You do a little thing in the back of your nose—like you're going to blow it—another little trick in the middle of the throat, and end with the good old American "Mom."

The children had already passed us in learning the language. Their Palauan friends could speak no English, so they had to quickly catch on in order to develop friendships. How thankful we were for all the people who were praying for their adjustment to a new life. God was abundantly answering those prayers, too!

Our article in the Liebenzell Mission publication read:

Yesterday we heard a loud, lively conversation coming from our showering place. We wondered who these Palauan kids were who were using our shower. Juanita went out to investigate. She found several little Palauan girls all talking at once, and the loudest one of all was ANGELA. They had been swimming and came in to get rinsed off. We are so pleased that Angela and Sandy are doing so well with the language. The Palauans say their pronunciation is excellent. This has opened hearts to us and to the gospel.

Angela has turned into a regular "mechas" (Palauan woman). Sometimes she goes to the taro swamps with the women. She comes back from "helping" in their smoky cookhouses smelling like a smoked fish. She prides herself in being able to squat down like a mechas and sweep the floor with an "oriik" (Palauan broom made from the stiff stems of palm fronds).

Sandy is becoming "kmal meduch" (very able) at fishing Palauan style. Almost every day after school he "mora chei" (goes fishing) out at the reef. This consists of diving down with a mask and spear gun to search under the coral rocks for the big ones. He keeps us well supplied with fish of all shapes, sizes and colors. Last week he and his friend Dulei speared a two-foot-long fish, big enough for our entire meal.

Pray for the children's schooling. Have you ever tried concentrating and doing your best work for several hours at the desk on the hottest day in August (without a fan or air conditioner)? Then you know what it's like for Sandy and Angela every day.

While our primary responsibility was as teachers in the Bethania High School, we also became more and more involved in village work. Excerpts from an article we wrote reflect our experiences of joy, disappointment, victory, and frustration.

Pray for the Christians of Ngersuul. We made a trip to this village on Palm Sunday weekend. Because of the tide, we were not able to get there until 9:30 Saturday night. The people insisted that we eat first, then have a meeting. So there we were with a "bai" (community house) full of people and only one gasoline lamp to break the darkness.

We had a wonderful time of fellowship. When our meeting ended at 11:30 P.M., the people were not ready to go home. Between the morning and afternoon services the next day, I was busy every minute with people who wanted to make decisions for Christ. Praise the Lord for the unusual eagerness of the people of Ngersuul to hear the gospel.

Our Easter began on Thursday morning with a 50-mile trip to Peleliu Island, taking nine and a half hours. On the way down we saw many beautiful and interesting sights—many little islands of indescribable beauty.

While we were at Peleliu we had eight services. We are sorry to report poor interest and attendance except for Friday and Saturday nights. What we lacked in backsliding adults we then more than made up in young people. On those evenings the church was full, with many more standing outside in the dark.

What do you suppose happened on Easter morning, just as we were about to begin the service? Two big dogs had a barking, brawling fight right in front of the pulpit! (Really nothing unusual here.) As they were whipping the dogs out of church, I thought, "What if this happened in one of our fashionable churches at home—on Easter Sunday morning!?"

Another more serious event happened earlier that weekend, as related by John in a special letter to children in our supporting churches.

What were you doing Good Friday afternoon? We were all sound asleep. You see, here in Palau at that time it was five o'clock Saturday morning, April 13th. The sun was just coming up over the island of Peleliu. The jungle birds and bats were still squawking and the air was strangely and pleasantly free of mosquitoes.

The silence was suddenly broken by Angela's voice in the next room: "Mommy, Mommy, it's hot!" Then there was the quick shuffling of bare feet and the urgent voice of Juanita calling, "Honey, come quickly! It's her mattress!" I stumbled half awake into the next room, to be sharply awakened by the near-choking smoke and a mattress alive with sparks. I'm not exactly sure even yet how I was able to gather the burning mattress in my arms and force it out the window. A place on the floor and a table leg were left still smoldering.

I still grow cold when I think how close we came to seeing Angela burned alive . . . not to mention all of us who peacefully slept in that termite-ridden Palauan house. In addition to our family, there were nine girls from our Senior Class in another room, and six of our Mission men and deacons in another. None of the fifteen people were aroused until I ran outside to control the flames.

As we stared down at the flaming mattress, we realized that the little spot on the edge where Angela had been sleeping was the only part not burning. There was nothing left of the sheet blanket that had been over her. Yet *not a hair* of her head was singed!

The mosquitoes had been so thick on our first night at Peleliu that we had been unable to sleep. So the second night we lit some mosquito coils and placed one on the floor a little distance away from Angela's mattress. (These coils are commonly used here. The smoke given off by them drives away the mosquitoes.) During the night she kicked off her sheet blanket and it fell over the smoldering little coil. There was enough smoke from that burning mattress to drive away all the mosquitoes in Palau!

Do you pray for Sandy and Angela? Maybe you prayed a special prayer for Angela on Good Friday afternoon. Now you know how God answered your prayer.

The more we traveled in the villages the more obvious it became that the congregations had grown cold. After thirty years of the gospel, the people of the villages were still waiting for the "missionary" to come. We felt that it was past time for a truly indigenous church. Back in the '40s, Palau's only two native pastors had been chosen to serve the churches during the war absence of the missionaries. Chelechuus and Albert were now old and physically handicapped. The villages of Palau desperately needed full-time Palauan pastors.

This great need of pastors and church workers caused us that first year of ministry to take a bold step toward preparation of new, young leaders. There were five young adults who were qualified and ready for further schooling, and eager to serve the Lord and the church on their return. The Lord graciously led us to hear about Far Eastern Bible Institute and

Seminary in Manila. We felt that our potential church leaders could be properly trained there in a culture somewhat similar to their own.

But there was no time to gather support for them. So, together with some of the other missionaries, we agreed to pool our slim personal resources in order to buy them plane tickets to Guam and Manila. Then we wrote our friends and asked them to help us with scholarship funds.

Thus began a period of many years in which Micronesian young people were sent to be trained at FEBIAS. Some were under scholarship and others went with personal funds. Today, many of the outstanding church leaders of Micronesia are those who were trained in Manila. The Lord proved that our concern for church leadership was really *His* concern, passed on to us!

8

THE THREE R'S AND MORE

"Thy sons shall come from far, and thy daughters shall be nursed at thy side."—Isa. 60:4b (KJV)

I had taught both the children for two and a half years when we began to realize that Sandy needed to be in a regular school. Already in seventh grade, he required something more in his schooling than his mother alone could give him. Scholastic achievement makes up only part of what we know of as "school." He needed the other parts.

Remembering the verse in Isaiah 60 about the children's future, I felt that perhaps the due time had arrived. We began writing letters to schools for missionaries' children of which we were familiar in our "neighborhood." Our neighborhood included Japan, Taiwan and the Philippines. Finally we found a school near Manila which sounded like an excellent possibility and almost within our limited budget. We wrote to Faith Academy for an application blank.

When the day arrived to send in the application, I simply couldn't do it. Laying it out before the Lord, I prayed, "This looks like a real good school, Lord, and I think it's the right one for Sandy. But I don't know for sure! I just cannot send off my pink-cheeked twelve-year-old unless I have confirmation from You. I don't know how You're going to do it, but somehow You must let me know that this is the school. You know me, Lord. If You tell me it's the right place, I'll send him off with perfect faith in Your choice."

Sometime before, I had been especially blessed by the study of chapter 49 of Isaiah. The Lord had brought to my attention many references to the future of both Sandy and me. Now my thoughts turned again to this chapter. Reading down from verse one, I stopped short at verse twelve. There were almost the same words that had been used in the prophecy in Isaiah 60: *"Behold, these shall come from far."* I read on. *"And, lo, these from the north and from the west; and these from the land of Sinim."*

I began to think of those directions. Directly northwest of Palau is Manila. Some of the Philippine Islands are directly west of Palau, but not Manila. "But," I thought, "Manila is not the only place northwest of Palau." Then I turned to *"the land of Sinim."* I remembered reading this before in the Word, but I had never stopped to find out what or where it was. Excitedly, I ran for the Bible dictionary. There it said something like this: "The land of Sinim is an ancient land relatively unknown. However, most Bible scholars believe it was a group of islands off the south coast of China."

Was it possible? Was God actually saying that Sandy would "come back" from the islands directly northwest of Palau and south of China? I laughed as I marveled at the miraculous ability of the Lord to pinpoint a place for me today from this ancient Book.

Still reveling in the clear-cut direction, I suddenly had another disquieting thought. "How do I know this is the year? I could teach Sandy his eighth-grade subjects. Wouldn't it be terrible if we sent him off a year early!" Then, returning to the same chapter, five verses further on I found that he should *"make haste."*[1]

Sandy expressed his feelings about the decision in a letter to friends:

> By the time you get this letter, I will be in Manila, the capital city of the Philippines. Dad, Mother and Angela are going with me to Guam. Then on July 19th I will fly alone to Manila on the jet.
>
> I guess you know that Mother has been our teacher for the last three years. She's not a bad teacher, but I think

---

[1] See principle #9, Appendix.

it will be kind of fun to be in a class with more than one pupil—ME! I'll probably miss my Palauan friends. I won't be able to have a pet like Mori at Faith Academy. But there will be lots of missionaries' kids there like me, so I'll be able to make some new friends. Then when I come back to Palau in the summer, I can go fishing again with Cot, Sep, and Hermino.

I suppose I'll have work to do there just like I do here. But that's O.K. Maybe if I save my money, I can get a bicycle like the one I had at Darlington. Boy! Don't forget to pray for me!

It was not easy for him or for us that day Sandy boarded the jet alone to fly to Manila. How we would have loved to accompany him to see him settled into a new school, a new country, a new way of life. But our tiny bank account could only manage a trip by small ship for all of us from Palau to Guam and one plane fare from Guam to Manila.

It was raining at the terminal in Guam when we saw Sandy off. The news had reported a typhoon in the Manila area. Rain and tears coursed together down our faces as we watched him bravely turn and wave good-bye. But deep inside was the warm assurance that this was the Lord's will, for He had selected the school and the time.

There were several times during the following years when I returned for assurance to the verses the Lord had given. When I missed Sandy more than I dared voice to anyone, I would look again at the words, *"come from far."* I was so thankful the Lord had not said, "go far away."

Living as we did on the island of Babeldaob where there were no roads, we also had no phone, no radio, no TV, no newspapers, and only very old magazines. Some of the Palauans in the nearby village of Ulimang had radios, so they would come to give us the news from time to time that they had heard on the Palauan news broadcast. "There's been a terrible earthquake in Manila" was the news one day reported by one of the villagers. "I heard many people died, and they said something about Sandy. I'm sure they said he died, too!"

WALKING THE WAVES

The informant was quite taken aback to see me smile and calmly assure him that he must be mistaken. "I think you misunderstood the news report. I'm sure that Sandy did not die." How could he know that I had a promise made years ago by an unfailing Father, that Sandy would *"come from far"*?[2]

I continued homeschooling Angela for the following three years (until we left on our first furlough). John wrote to our relatives:

> Angela is a good girl and doing a very good job on her schoolwork. Last weekend she was surprised to have her friend Jan Thompson, daughter of an American teacher from the northern end of Babeldaob, visit her. Jan was born again when we visited her village last Easter. She says that she wants to be a missionary, much to the displeasure of her unbelieving parents.
>
> The minute she arrived she wanted to play Sunday School with Angela, and play it they did, complete with flannelgraph stories and songs, and the children of the village joining in. Pray for this poor little rich girl, starved for the things that are real. Angela, of course, was teaching the lesson smoothly as could be in flawless Palauan, and then translating it into fifth-grade English so that Jan could understand it. Pray for our little missionary, too!

Angela had said at eight years of age that she planned to be a missionary when she grew up. She would always watch and listen closely when I taught Sunday School to the Palauan children in the villages. One day she came with a request: "Mom, do you think that I could make a small flannelboard and some little figures so that I can tell stories like you do?"

"Why not?" I answered. "Let's look for a piece of flannel and make a little board. I think I have some small figures in my collection of Bible story flannel figures. Let's see what we can do."

Thus began Angela's career as a missionary. She soon was

---

[2] See principle #10, Appendix.

out in the neighborhood calling the children together. They congregated under a tree, eagerly anticipating a "chel-dececheduch" (story or lesson). Angela taught them some children's songs, told them a Bible story, and led them in prayer. From then on she often gathered the children in the nearby villages to teach them about the Lord.

Angela had many close friends among the children of Ngesang and Ulimang where we lived. But her closest chum was Dora Maui, daughter of one of the deacons. We wrote to my father in December 1966: "Angela and her friend Dora are busily learning their Palauan recitations for the Christmas program. They have sent for 'osoroi' (matching) dresses, and they're hoping that the ship will deliver them in time. They have been singing duets in church on Sunday evenings lately. Angela teaches Dora the tune and English words. Then when Dora has learned it well, Angela sings the alto with her. They sound like a couple of Christmas angels!"

Christmas for Sandy was harder since we couldn't afford to bring him home from the Philippines. We wrote: "Sandy will be visiting some kind family in Manila again this Christmas. He has recently made the Junior Varsity Basketball Team, and has been promoted to the Senior Band (as mellophonist). How terribly we miss him! But we daily praise the Lord for providing this excellent Christian school as a step in his training to serve the Lord with his life."

Our Christmas was a busy one, with lots of meetings scheduled. One of the joys of Christmas in Palau those days was the centrality of Christ and the church in the Christmas celebrations. It is culturally appropriate for Palauans to celebrate big events, so Christmas was a time for different villages to gather and enjoy fellowship, food and worship together. Since the only two Palauan pastors were getting old and found it difficult to travel much, the people often asked for us to be present if possible at their "Christmas event."

That year we spent December 24th and 25th flying in the speedboat to three different villages to celebrate the "Christmas event" with the nine village groups gathered. On the 26th we came back home on the noon tide to celebrate our own family Christmas.

Our burden for years had been for all of Micronesia, and in the summer of 1964 we had our first opportunity to visit some of the islands east of the Palau chain. We were asked to represent the missionaries stationed on Palau at a Missionary and Indigenous Leaders Conference taking place in Pohnpei.

We had a wonderful "cruise" almost 2000 miles directly east, and a month later while returning straight west from Pohnpei. We traveled one way on the *Gunner's Knot* and the other on the *Pacific Islander*. Although freighters, they were larger than the little *Errol* on which we had voyaged before. We actually had our own cabin! And the food was delicious, especially after our limited island diet. The seas were calm and the weather gorgeous. The ship travel provided a very special vacation for us as a family.

The Lord used this time to increase our burden, showing us some of the specific needs on other islands. We passed by and sighted a couple of the outer Yap Islands, feeling pain as we remembered once again that there was no gospel witness on those tiny, isolated bits of land. It was on this trip that we met some of the missionaries and nationals with whom I worked many years later. We fellowshiped with Liebenzell and United Church of Christ missionaries from Chuuk (formerly Truk), Pohnpei (formerly Ponape), and Kosrae (formerly Kusaie), and met many church leaders from various areas of Micronesia.

We experienced two unusual blessings on that trip. John had unique opportunities after the conference was over while we were waiting for the delayed ship to arrive. He was asked to preach to several congregations around the island of Pohnpei. We fell in love with the Kapingamarangi people, who all stood up at the invitation. John told them to sit down while he began again from the beginning to explain the gospel and the seriousness of commitment to Christ. When he finished they all stood again!

The second blessing was in the form of new Bethania girls

from Pohnpei, Kosrae and Chuuk who traveled back to Palau with us on the ship. Their parents came begging us to take them with us so that they could attend Bethania High School. One girl was 21, but she had not attended school past sixth grade because her father wouldn't let her go to school due to the "evil influences" there. Another girl, already 20 years old, cried a lot on the ship. Her brother was one of the sailors, so he comforted her by saying that he would pay her way back to Pohnpei if she would stick it out at Bethania for the year. She dried her tears, and spent the next six years (from seventh to twelfth grades) with us at Bethania without ever going home! She wrote to her parents that she had found a home away from home.

Excerpts from letters to my father highlight some of the problems, joys and disappointments that we were encountering in those early years on the field.

March 1965: "*Satan, a Defeated Foe* [3] has been a real blessing to me. The Lord has revived my heart through it and won a significant victory over Satan in my life. I have had a real struggle with early morning devotions. Praise the Lord for His victory over the already defeated foe!

". . . The Lord led me to translate five new songs for Easter for my hymn-singing class to learn (it's the whole school). It's my first attempt at lengthy translation of something permanent. Those whom I asked said they are good. I'm not so sure. I think they are only passable. Pray that the Lord will use them this Easter anyway."

June 1965: "I think if some people could really see our situation, they would think that we have lost our minds. By faith, we are accepting all students. Of course, we have one less high school teacher this year with Elsbeth Reumann gone. We have to remodel and replace wood on our termite-ridden sewing and typing room to make it into another dorm room. We have to use our house, Wanda Aigner's house (which is ready to collapse from termites), and our workers' house as

---

[3] Charles H. Usher, *Satan, a Defeated Foe* or *How to Enter into Christ's Victory over Satan*; Fort Washington, PA, Christian Literature Crusade, 1964.

temporary classrooms. We have to buy more books, beds, lockers, etc., for the new students. Meanwhile, we are trying to move ahead with our new building which will house classrooms and be residence for the women missionaries. We only have five men workers, and one of them is always busy on the boat or fixing motors. All of this on just barely enough money to pay the workers and meet running expenses of the school! Well, time will tell whether we are just gigantic fools or we have a gigantic Lord!"

December 1965: "We have been waiting for definite word about the new missionaries recruited at Schooley's Mountain. They (Herb and Sylvia Lange) are coming here—maybe this month. This is a wonderful answer to some desperate prayers. They have two small children, so we decided that the old house in which Wanda and Elsbeth have been living would not be suitable for them. So, on top of everything else, we decided to move over to this old house, in order to vacate our house for them and Wanda. It's in much better shape and much bigger—to say nothing of the better toilet and shower. I wish that we had movies of the girls moving all our stuff that day. Wanda's went one way and ours the other. This house where we have moved is completely termite-ridden. It's a job to keep the old floors and underpinnings patched up enough to walk on. Since our refrigerator and stove are big and heavy, we left them there for the Langes to use and we're trying to keep this old stove and refrigerator going."

February 1966: "Where else in the world do you suppose this could happen: A student came up to Juanita after one of her English classes and said, 'Sometime when you're free, could I come to your house and be born again?' This is what comes from having a school that is Christ-centered."

May 1966: "Please pray for our financial situation. The money the Mission sent us for the new building has been used. Now we have nothing, and we need more materials right away. Herb thinks that he will be sent to Emmaus [the boys' high school in Koror] when Al and Carol [Froelich] go on furlough next year. That means that we have his help only till then. Pray that we'll have enough materials to keep him going. We already have many applications for girls who want to attend next year. Since the building is still quite a ways from completion, we will have to turn away many girls."

March 1967: "Despite the use of many medicines and remedies, my intestinal condition has grown steadily worse, requiring me to go to the Naval Hospital in Guam." From Guam, I wrote to my father after ten days of tests, x-rays and examinations: "It's Friday morning and I can give you the doctor's report. He said that they couldn't find anything physically wrong through all the tests. He thinks it is just a case of my body not being able to take the strain any longer. He says I have pushed myself too hard and for too long.

". . . He gave me medicine and said that I must try to delegate some of my responsibilities to others if possible; that John and I should try to get away for a vacation; and that I should find ways to take a break in my long days of mental work. I'm thankful for the doctor's report. I'm sure that he initially felt it was cancer. I think the Lord wanted to warn us to do something about our pace before it is too late."

And so, the needs and problems continued year after year, and the blessings poured down from the hand of a gracious God, though not always on the timetable we would have chosen. *"'Test Me in this,' says the Lord Almighty, 'and see if I will not throw open the floodgates of heaven and pour out so much blessing that you will not have room enough for it.'"*—Mal. 3:10b.

9

SINGING IN THE DARKNESS

"The blessing of the Lord, it maketh rich, and He addeth no sorrow with it."—Prov. 10:22 (KJV)

That other prophecy about the future came to my mind often. I had long since reconciled myself to John's death, but sometimes I would weep at night as I realized that the years were slipping by, bringing that unwelcome event ever closer. One day it dawned on me that I was worrying about how he would die. "Lord," I prayed, "You have used John's life as a great blessing to many people. I want his death to be a testimony to You as well."

Remembering how miraculously the Lord had put His finger on a date and a place in the past, I decided to ask Him the question: "Lord, will You tell me how John will die? It will put my anxiety to rest."

Several days passed.[1] I was doing my daily devotional reading in Ezekiel. One night as I read chapter 28, the answer jumped out at me from the second half of verse 8: *"And you will die a violent death in the heart of the seas."* Later the Lord tenderly spoke to me from Isaiah 57:1–2a (KJV): *"The righteous perisheth, and no man layeth it to heart: and merciful men are taken away, none considering that the righteous is taken away from the evil to come. He shall enter into peace."*

With the special loving preparation the Lord had given, it is not surprising that the shock of John's death, when it came, was not as great for me as for others.

So it was, that Friday morning on the eighth of Septem-

---

[1] See principle #11, Appendix.

ber in 1967, that the Lord kept me from sinking into the depths of heartbreak and despair. Sitting at the little straight-backed desk in the classroom where we gathered each morning for devotions, I looked out at the golden sky—once again lit up like the New Jerusalem itself with the glory of the rising sun. As the sky brought the hope of a new day today and a glorious eternity tomorrow, so God's Word brought the glow of hope to my heart. For I believed that the One who had *"promised"* would also *"perform"* (Rom. 4:21, KJV) all those wonderful promises He had made for the children and me—and for our beloved islands.

When on Wednesday morning John had left, I had no premonition of danger. I thought as I always did when he went out in the boat, "One of these times will be the last." But I never felt morose about it. After all, I had committed John to the Lord's will many years before, and each time I thought of the future I simply recommitted both John and myself to His perfect plan, though usually with tears.

I was busy with a thousand last-minute details that morning. The next day would be the first day of the new school year. Our principal had been on furlough for fifteen months. She was due to return but had not yet arrived. John had been working night and day to complete the new addition to the dining room and to finish enough of the classrooms and the dormitory so that they might be used for our increased enrollment. This left all the details of the principal's job to me.

"Hon, I'm going to have to go to Koror," were the words that I heard. Looking up, I saw John standing outside the classroom where the girls and I were arranging desks.

Glancing toward the shore, I said, "Isn't it too late? It looks as though the tide is already going out."

"Yes, it is, but I think I can make it if I leave right now. I have some errands I must do before school starts."

"Will you be able to be back for your classes tomorrow morning?" I asked anxiously.

"Sure. I'll be back tonight. That's why I'm going today, so that I won't have to miss classes after school starts," John assured me. "But I've got to run now!" he added, looking toward the receding water.

Leaving the classroom, I said, "I'll come down and see you off. Don't you want a sandwich to take with you? I can make one real fast."

"Never mind, dear, I'm not hungry. But listen, you've got to do something for me," he insisted urgently. "The men are waiting to use the electric saw. You know they don't know how to work the big generator, so you must go out and start it. First, though, it has to be filled with diesel. I took the fuel filter out this morning to clean it. You'll have to put it back before you fill it."

"Boy, I hope I can do it all right," I said anxiously. "You know I don't know much about that generator, hon, and I sure would hate to have anything happen to it."

"Don't worry. Just do what I showed you last week. But you'll have to do it right now because they are all standing around waiting. And I've got to leave." The last words faded out as he turned hurriedly toward the beach. "I'll see you tonight, dear," he called over his shoulder.

It took me several minutes to fix the filter, fill the tank, and start the generator. Coming out of the semidarkness of the generator building, I looked toward the shore. I could just see the orange top of our new little speedboat, *Faith,* contrasted against the azure sea as John turned south toward Koror. I never guessed that that evening he would make his very last journey through the wet, cold darkness into the eternal light and warmth of the Savior's arms.

When John didn't return that evening I wasn't concerned. He often stayed longer than he had expected to in Koror because of the bank being closed or some similar reason. Besides, the high tide was late that night. It was dark early, with heavy rain and unusually strong wind. The waves were rougher than usual. I reasoned that he had decided to spend the night in Koror and would be home on the morning tide.

I knew that the tide would not be high enough for the speedboat to come in until after 9 A.M., so the next morning I went to John's classes to give them assignments to work on. Then I taught Angela, prepared and taught my own classes—always with one ear attuned to the sound of the speedboat motor. By noon I knew it was too late for the boat to come in. After our faculty prayer meeting, I went out to the generator building to start the generator. I had decided to try to call the missionaries in Koror on our single-sideband radio.

The generator started with no trouble as it had the day before. But when I tried to engage the lighting mechanism, it wouldn't work. I tried over and over to make it light, without success. Finally, realizing that it was time for classes to begin again, I gave up.

In the evening the girls called me to say that a Palauan diesel boat had arrived. I waded into the water to meet it, finding out from the boatsman that John had hired him in Koror to bring a load of lumber up for the new building.

"Where is Pastor?" the boatsman asked in Palauan.

"I don't know," I answered. "He hasn't returned yet. Haven't you seen him?"

"The last time I saw him was yesterday afternoon at the dock in Koror. But he said he planned to leave for home in a couple of hours. I'm sure he left. What could have happened to him?" he said, his brow cut with lines of deep concern.

Turning, I ran once again to the generator building. "Somehow I must get that generator going," I thought. "Lord, help me to get it to light!"

The generator started and lit. I ran over to my fellow missionary's room where the radio cabinet was located. She wasn't in her room, so I went in and turned on the radio. As soon as it warmed up I realized that it was probably a useless attempt because the static was so loud. I was sure the missionaries in Koror would never hear me. But I tried anyway.

As I stood at the radio, calling and waiting for an answer . . . calling and waiting for an answer . . . my eyes fell on something I had not noticed before. Though I had been in Elsbeth Reumann's room many times, I had not seen it until now. There, beside the radio cabinet, was a wooden plaque.

As I stared at it, the words suddenly became alive. They were the same words that had brought me as a girl of twelve into the family of God: *"I will never leave you nor forsake you."*— Heb. 13:5b. Although I never reached Koror that night, I had my answer.

Friday morning I was awakened early by a rat running across my legs. I didn't want to be late to morning devotions, so I shut him up in my bedroom with the warning that I would be back to kill him later. After devotions, I went once again to the generator building. With both the generator and radio operating fine, I managed finally to reach Sylvia Lange in Koror. In answer to my question, I heard her shocked counter-question: "Didn't he get home? You mean from his trip two days ago? He left here Wednesday evening at six!"

As soon as the tide was high enough, missionary Herb Lange and Palauan pastor Hubert Charles started out from Koror, stopping at the villages to inquire for John. Other small boats from our village and Koror joined in the search. When Herb and Hubert arrived at Bethania to take Angela and me to Koror, I told them that I thought John was gone and why. Herb, however, simply couldn't accept the possibility of John's death.

I called Angela into the house, explaining that as yet no one had seen a sign of Daddy and we must go to Koror, where we could receive up-to-date news of the search. She began to sob uncontrollably, so I asked her to tell me about that glorious Home where her father had gone, if he were not found again on this earth. She quieted immediately, obviously committing herself and her Dad to the hands of the Savior—whom she had come to know personally when only six, in one of her father's evangelistic meetings in Indiana. How it thrilled my heart to see her calm, sweet spirit through the days and weeks that followed.

During the two-hour speedboat trip to Koror the men were constantly on the lookout for a boat or wreckage—or a body. Once, as we passed some uninhabited rock islands, Herb saw a small speedboat coming toward us. "It looks like the *Faith!*"

he exclaimed excitedly. "Maybe he had to stay on one of those islands for some reason. Look! Isn't that John? It looks like him!" But of course it wasn't.

Sitting quietly with Angela's head in my lap, I mused at how we all loved the sea. I drank in again the beauty of the clear blue sky, the mushrooms of green which were the rock islands, and the ever-changing sea. It was rough even now, and I thought of how very rough it must have been last Wednesday night for the lone man traveling through the darkness. Strangely enough, I felt neither fear nor resentment toward our beautiful and powerful Pacific. I knew that the rest of my life would be spent on the islands in this very ocean if the Lord would give me that privilege.

As always, my mind turned to the Word. Now, more than ever, it was the lifeline to which I must cling, with nothing more than my faith in the One who spoke it to keep me afloat. The verses I had read the past two days followed one another, single file, through my head.

> "The eternal God is thy refuge, and underneath are the everlasting arms."—Deut. 33:27a (KJV).
>
> "He will swallow up death in victory; and the Lord God will wipe away tears from off all faces."—Isa. 25:8a (KJV).
>
> "Who shall separate us from the love of Christ? Shall trouble or hardship or persecution or famine or nakedness or danger or sword? As it is written: 'For Your sake we face death all day long; we are considered as sheep to be slaughtered.' No, in all these things we are more than conquerors through Him who loved us. For I am convinced that **neither death nor life**, neither angels nor demons, **neither the present nor the future**, nor any powers, neither height nor depth, nor anything else in all creation, will he able to separate us from the love of God that is in Christ Jesus our Lord."—Rom. 8:35–39.
>
> "He shall not be afraid of evil tidings; his heart is fixed, trusting in the Lord."—Psa. 112:7 (KJV).
>
> "Who is wise? He will realize these things. Who is discerning? He will understand them. The ways of the Lord are

right; the righteous walk in them, but the rebellious stumble in them."—Hosea 14:9.

"The steps of a good man are ordered by the Lord."—Psa. 37:23a (KJV).

"Thou shalt increase my greatness, and comfort me on every side."—Psa. 71:21 (KJV).

"Though He brings grief, He will show compassion, so great is His unfailing love."—Lam. 3:32.

"They shall lift up their voice, they shall sing for the majesty of the Lord, they shall cry aloud from the sea. Wherefore, **glorify ye the Lord in the fires,** *even the name of the Lord God of Israel* **in the isles of the sea.** *From the uttermost part of the earth have we heard* **songs,** *even glory to the righteous."*—Isa. 24:14–16a (KJV).

I had difficulty restraining laughter and song as I meditated on these beautiful verses and reveled in the all-pervading peace which engulfed my being. God had promised a peace that the world cannot give or take away, and I was experiencing that peace in its fullness simply through submission to the will of the Father.

In October I wrote a letter to my close relatives, in which I explained things that were not generally known. The first three years of our ministry John was quite well, but he had begun to have increasing problems with angina the last couple of years. He had refused to see a doctor about it. I think he felt that a doctor would tell him to quit all that he was doing, and he was unwilling to save himself. Perhaps, though he never mentioned it, he knew that his time on earth was short. He was determined to use whatever was left to its fullest. The last few months of his life, he literally lived on nitroglycerine pills. The children and I were often amazed at his perseverance and determination in light of the pain that we knew he was dealing with. I wrote:

> You have all asked how John really was. Well, neither of us was in very good shape. You already know about my condition in the spring. We said nothing about

John, because he wouldn't allow it. Besides, I guess he figured there was no point talking about it because the only thing that could be done for him was to tell him to stop. Since he had no intention of doing that, why talk about it?

Actually John's heart condition has been growing steadily worse. No one knew about it, but I knew the increasing number of nitroglycerine pills he was taking. I tried to encourage him to rest when he could, but that was seldom. I stopped nagging him years ago because I realized that he must use his life the way he saw best, doing what he felt the Lord wanted him to do.

We both had a nice change and some rest in Guam. However, it wasn't a vacation by a long shot. We were very busy with many speaking engagements and looking for and packing all kinds of supplies for the school and the new building. It meant a lot of heavy lifting and lugging, which none of us was really able to do. Sandy was such a big help, but he strained his back in the process. In spite of that, we returned feeling much better. But then, when we got back, we were faced with a mountain of work that had to be finished before school could be opened. So I had another setback and John just took more pills.

John was extremely tired the day he went to Koror. No one knows what happened because his body and the things in the boat have not been found, and probably will not be. Many of our dear Palauan friends kept searching in their boats and diving every day for over a week. I personally feel that one of two things probably happened.

Since it was quite rough and dark when it happened, I think that he may have hit a big wave which he couldn't see coming. If you don't hit those big ones just right, it's too bad. If he hit wrong, he could have been tossed right out of the boat. Or he might have had a bad heart pain because of the rough trip and fallen overboard. I think that something like this happened because the five typewriters were not found inside the reef. Probably the boat went on without him, and was turned over when it got into the big reef waves. That would toss the typewriters, etc., over the reef into the deep water where they would not be found. There is one thing I'm sure of: John did not live long after he hit the water. I would say that he probably died immediately, because the sudden shock of being thrown out was all his tired heart could take.

With what joy he must have met his Savior, finally free of all pain, problems, and trials. How can I possibly be sad to think of his great and everlasting joy in the presence of our dear Savior. As I know the Lord would not have taken him unless his work was done, I cannot regret anything. There are no second causes in the center of God's will. And how thankful I am that John wanted to spend himself till the end. How awful if he had died in an easy chair in the U.S., trying to take care of himself so as to prolong his life. John wanted to die in the throes of the fight and he did. I pray that the Lord will grant me the same privilege. Nor could I ask any greater heritage for Sandy and Angela than this.

I can't tell you how extremely minute the things of this world seem to me. In Guam, so many times I found myself listening to a conversation about "things." I felt like a detached observer listening to something with which I have no connection. It was almost like watching a colony of ants working like mad to gather a few crumbs.

I wish that I could somehow describe for you the depth of the peace that has kept my heart. It's beyond description! I think that some people think that I am sort of riding on the crest and one of these days I'll fall into the abyss. But that's not what the Lord's promise said to me: *"Neither shall the covenant of My peace be removed, saith the Lord that hath mercy on thee."*—Isa. 54:10b (KJV). The Lord knows that I certainly don't rest in my own strength. I don't have any to rest in. It's the Lord's work and His peace, so there's no fear for the future.

I think the young men in the boat wondered about the

smile they saw on my face. Perhaps they thought I was hoping where there was no hope. The next day the deacons who saw that smile were pained and offended. They knew that the District Administrator had given me the news just an hour before. The ship and plane search had finally been successful in finding the *Faith* fifteen miles offshore. It was upside down, with the motor still turned on though not running. There were no signs of the boat's contents or John. Palauans were still diving in the area where they felt John had been thrown overboard or the boat had capsized. Nothing was ever found.

On my way down to the Radio Shack to send telegrams to relatives and the Mission, I saw three Palauan deacons and smiled. That afternoon they came, motivated by both sympathy and curiosity, to the Langes' house where we were staying. I sat down with them to explain the verses of the past six years, and why I was not shocked at John's death. I told them that my earnest prayer was found in Psalm 27:11: *"Teach me Thy way, O Lord, and lead me in a plain path, because of those which observe me."* [2]

"We were among those observing you, and we saw a smile. We were hurt and offended because we didn't understand. Now we see that all you and Pastor Simpson have been teaching us is *true*. We know now that God's promises are real, for we see them in your life—even through this dark valley. We have never seen anyone face death like this before. You will be a blessing to all Palau," they assured me, "as our people see that Christianity is not just words."

Through the days that followed, the Lord fulfilled the prediction of the three deacons.

---

[2] Literal translation of the Hebrew, according to 1611 KJV footnote.

10

DRY EYES AND TEARS OF JOY

"These all died in faith, not having received the promises, but having seen them afar off, and were persuaded of them, and embraced them, and confessed that they were strangers and pilgrims on the earth. For they that say such things declare plainly that they seek a country. And truly, if they had been mindful of that country from whence they came out, they might have had opportunity to have returned. But now they desire a better country, that is, an heavenly: wherefore God is not ashamed to be called their God: for He hath prepared for them a city."—Heb. 11:13–16 (KJV)

*M*any responsibilities fell on my shoulders with John's passing. That big generator was only one of many motors and machines about which our Palauan workers knew little or nothing. The new building was still uncompleted. The treasurer's job promised to be most challenging, as the treasury had already hit bottom and now the loss of five typewriters, $600 in cash, a Billy Graham film, and numerous unknown supplies in the speedboat had to be subtracted from nothing. These and the many other problems facing me I simply laid at the Savior's feet, reminding Him daily of my incapabilities and making Him responsible. I had only three real concerns.

The first was *revival in Micronesia.* We had been praying for the Lord's work in this group of 2100 islands of the Pacific since our first introduction to them (by name only) fifteen years before. In the past five years we had been privileged to serve at the Bethania School where we had girls from all over Micronesia. With our increased knowledge of this whole island world and better understanding of the language and transportation problems involved in reaching these tiny scattered outposts, the burden grew. Now I had many verses underlined in my Bible which I believed to be specific promises regarding the future of the work. Up to this time, the fulfillment of many of these promises seemed to be somehow contingent on John.

The Lord gave my questioning heart rest from this burden while answering my second concern. It was more immediate. As I recalled the evangelistic sermons John had preached and the hundreds who had responded to his invitations, my heart sank. Even the night before he died, the Lord had given him fruit as four of our new students had made a decision for Christ at John's invitation.

Al Froelich, with whom we had served for four of our five years in Palau, summarized the impact of John's missionary career at the Memorial Service held at Liebenzell Mission headquarters in New Jersey on Sunday, October 1, 1967:

"The first time we saw the Simpsons was on the day they arrived in Palau. With the Emmaus boys, we went to the dock to watch them come in on the small old freighter. As the ship drew nearer, we had our first glimpse of four smiling faces that were to become so familiar to us.

"As the Simpsons disembarked, we began singing 'This world is not my home, I'm just a-passing through,' and of course the musical Simpsons joined in. The message of this song characterized the life of John Simpson and his ministry on the islands. This world was not his home. For him it was a place of great need, a place of opportunity, a place for service —to be taken advantage of while there was still time and strength.

"While Brother Simpson served at Bethania Seminary, the school reached new heights in many areas. Its high academic standards were well known throughout Micronesia. In the physical realm, new buildings were constructed, making it possible for a much more efficient operation of the mission station.

"However, it was in the spiritual realm that Brother

Simpson became most endeared to those to whom he ministered. Under his ministry many girls were born again by the Holy Spirit. They were challenged to become witnesses in their villages and far-away islands. When he visited other areas of Palau and Micronesia, great blessings accompanied his preaching and many were brought into a new relationship to their Lord and Savior.

"'Work for the night is coming!' Brother Simpson could not rest as long as there was work to do. He is remembered as one who was always ready to speak a word for the Lord, whenever opportunity arose. He was not mindful of physical danger, nor did he seek worldly comfort or 'the easy life.' It was because of this attitude that he set forth in his boat that last day, desiring to return to the place where his many responsibilities awaited him.

"During World War II, a chaplain who went off to the service, and subsequent death, told his father, 'Don't pray that I might be saved. Pray that I might be *adequate*.' This was the prayer and the desire of our departed brother. May the example of his life and ministry result in renewed dedication and fruitfulness in all our lives. The Lord has left us here a little while longer, to carry on in the same work so ably done by John Simpson."

•   •   •

My heart cry was: "Now who will take his place, Lord? We have many new students at both the Bethania Girls' School and Emmaus Boys' School, to say nothing of all the unsaved villagers. Who will preach the messages that will lead them to the cross?"

On a previous Sunday night there had been a Memorial Service in Koror. The church was packed with Christians of several denominations as well as many unbelievers. Hearts were moved as they heard John's testimony on tape.

That evening after the Memorial Service, I sensed the Lord's urging that I should speak to the young men of Emmaus the next morning. It hardly seemed proper, but I finally agreed, and asked the principal's permission to speak to the boys. Yet I was somehow unable to prepare. I tried to make notes, but I just kept hearing, "Don't worry about it. I'll give you the message when the time comes."

I don't even remember now what the message consisted of. I only know that the Lord spoke, and as the Spirit moved hearts, 40 of the 65 young men present indicated a desire to know Christ. That was only the beginning. Through the ensuing weeks and months we saw many others respond for salvation and dedication of their lives—not just through my messages, but through the messages and invitations of missionaries and nationals, men and women alike.

Finally I realized that Abraham, too, had *"died in faith, not having received the promises."*—Heb. 11:13 (KJV). This certainly did not void all that God had said would come to pass. The most amazing and exciting thing of all was to understand that our almighty God can use anyone—*even me!* His power is only hindered when we are not the humble clay to be molded as He sees fit.

Then I saw that God's work would go on—to the conversion of many souls in Palau and all over Micronesia, until there were *"so many as the stars of the sky in multitude, and as the sand which is by the seashore innumerable"* (Heb. 11:12, KJV)—just as He had promised that memorable night of November 12, 1961.

My third concern was more personal. I had been skimming over those "waves" for a week and a half, like the eagle of Psalm 103:5,[1] while the Lord satisfied my heart with *"good things"* out of His Word. Typical of His tenderness was the day I found the verse in John's coat pocket.

It was Tuesday morning. Monday evening we had had the second Memorial Service, up at Bethania for the schoolgirls and villagers unable to travel to Koror.

The tears had streamed freely and the sobbing had been audible as the girls met us on the beach Monday afternoon.

---

[1] *"He satisfies your desires with good things, so that your youth is renewed like the eagle's."* (KJV)

Confused by our radiant smiles, they listened in hushed silence while I told them of the promise in Isaiah 25:8,[2] and how the Lord had already given victory in the hearts of their brothers and cousins at Emmaus who had been born again that very morning. "Now you see that the Lord has wiped away our tears," I concluded. "But He promised to wipe away tears from off all faces, so let Him dry yours, too."

I could hear the note of victory that night in the songs sung by the girls under the beautiful banner they had made, which read:

"Only one life, 'twill soon be past;
Only what's done for Christ will last!"[3]

Tuesday morning, the visiting missionaries had to return to their stations. I knew that Herb Lange and Wilhelm Fey would be able to wear some of John's clothes, and I wanted them to have them. I went to the closet where I had hung the garment bag which contained his good suit. The last time he had worn it was on the 9000-mile trip from the States five years earlier.

Going through the pockets of his coat, I found only tracts. I had to stop a moment with moist eyes to thank the Lord for giving me such a man to love for almost twenty-five years.

In one pocket I found a small capsule which I recognized as a "gospel bomb." As teenagers, John and I had often thrown these out of the car onto the sidewalk, hoping that someone would be attracted to the bright plastic capsule, pick it up, and read the Bible verse rolled up inside. The plastic was broken, so I pulled out the little roll of paper and read: *"And the peace of God, which passeth all understanding, shall keep your hearts and minds through Christ Jesus."*—Phil. 4:7 (KJV).

•   •   •

So I had skimmed the water as if on the wings of an eagle. Then suddenly my eagle wings faltered. Fluttering down, I

[2] *"He will swallow up death in victory; and the Lord God will wipe away tears from off all faces."* (KJV)
[3] Author unknown.

saw with Peter what cannot be seen—*"the wind boisterous"*—
and began to sink.

Our principal, Wanda Aigner, had arrived from furlough.
Knowing she had passed through Manila, I could hardly wait
to ask her about Sandy. It had been very difficult not being
able to talk with him—for there was no phone communication with the Philippines at that time. Because I had felt that a
short telegram would be a great shock to him, I had decided
to write a long letter instead, thinking he would receive it
within a week.

The great black cloud descended as I sat, transfixed, listening to Wanda's story: "I had sent Sandy a telegram of sympathy from Germany. Of course, he hadn't had time to receive any word from you, and the telegram only confused
him. He didn't understand it. He was having his semester
exams that week—and his teachers said that it had been difficult for him to take exams, not knowing whether his Dad was
alive or dead. I got to the school on Thursday, his fifteenth
birthday. So, of course, it was my job to give him the news."

"What was his reaction? Did he say anything?" I whispered.

"No. He just sat there and cried."

I just couldn't bear the thought of it. There was my only
son, in the middle of exam week, on his birthday, 2200 flight
miles from home, and not even a comforting word from his
mother. "Lord, this is too much," I cried in my heart. "Why
should he have to suffer so? It just isn't fair."

From out of the blue into my memory came that life-sav-
ing verse: *"And all thy children shall be taught of the Lord; and
great shall be the peace of thy children."*—Isa. 54:13 (KJV).[4] I
grabbed it and hung on with all the faith I had. The storm
clouds lifted as I heard the voice of Jesus say, "It is I. I am the
Great Teacher. You must trust Me to teach your children all
the lessons I know they need to learn, even those difficult
lessons of suffering. Haven't you come to appreciate *'The treasures of darkness and hidden riches of secret places'* [5] which I have

---

[4] See principle #12, Appendix.
[5] Isa. 45:3a (KJV).

given you in suffering? You must understand that your children, too, need these lessons if they are to become My faithful servants. I must prepare them for the great work for Me that they will do. I have promised to them the greatest gift in this world—My peace. You have seen this peace on Angela's smiling face. Now you simply must believe that Sandy, too, will have it."[6]

And he did. Three weeks passed before I received his first letter. By faith I knew what it would say, but the tears of joy fell as I read: "When I heard about Dad, it really struck home. People all around have been praying for me and I have had a strange peace in my heart. . . . I'm really going to have to start moving in my Christian life. I went to the street meeting today and I talked to a very stubborn man, but I felt better afterwards. . . . Tell me what is happening in Palau over Dad's death. I'm praying, just like Dad used to do, that this will start a revival in Palau. . . . Tell Angela that if she cried, not to be discouraged, because I cried, too! But just remember that Dad went to heaven, and we want to do everything we can to see him again when the time comes. But we must carry on what he did until Jesus comes and all pain and sorrow are gone!"

Almost two years later while we were on furlough, visiting in Germany, Sandy composed his first song, which reflected his thoughts about this painful time and the hope we have for tomorrow:

"I Know"

I know I'm going to a better place to stay;
I know that there, instead of night it's day;
And I know that somewhere beyond tomorrow
There'll be a place just built for me.
Oh, I have waited what seems like forever
for Him to come and take me away.
When I'm impatient, then I remember
that He did so much for me.

---

[6] See principle #13, Appendix.

WALKING THE WAVES

Now I know that there's a place inside
where the Holy Spirit burns.
I know I'll serve Him till the day that He returns;
And I know that somewhere beyond tomorrow
There'll be a place just built for me.

11

Only Temporary

"Therefore we do not lose heart. Though outwardly we are wasting away, yet inwardly we are being renewed day by day. For our light and momentary troubles are achieving for us an eternal glory that far outweighs them all. So we fix our eyes not on what is seen, but on what is unseen. For what is seen is temporary, but what is unseen is eternal."—2 Cor. 4:16–18

*O*ne day as I traveled back to Bethania on our slow boat, I was thinking about John. I was remembering with a touch of wistfulness his wonderful sense of humor. One of his favorite expressions came to my mind. Since we seldom had the real materials or tools needed for jobs, much of the patch-up work was regarded as only temporary until we could maybe someday get the real thing. John invented an expression which everyone took up and used: "Ngdi temborari!" (It's only temporary). It always produced laughter when we used this, as it was so apropos to our lifestyle.

As I sat there on the prow of the boat alone, I thought of how true this is of our world. Everything is "only temporary." Then I realized that all the hard and dark things with which we deal are also "only temporary." They will pass away. As long as we are exiles on this earth, we will be *"wasting away"* outwardly but inwardly we can be *"renewed day by day."* What we must do is keep our eyes on the *"eternal glory"* which is *"unseen."* That day I wrote a little song, entitled:

"Only Temporary"

Clouds are only temporary—dark skies, too!
Trouble's only temporary. Why should it make me blue?

Chorus: I've got the Lord beside me, and He's the One
who'll guide me
Every day, all the way—past the golden sunset, up
to the crystal sea.
There I'll meet my loved ones and my Jesus I shall
see.

2. Tears are only temporary—soon be dry.
Heartache's only temporary. There's no need to cry!

3. Pain is only temporary—'twill be past.
Death is only temporary! I'll be at Home at last.

Coda: Everything is temporary, soon be gone.
Jesus gives me peace and joy that goes on and
on and on.

Soon after John's death, I received a letter from the Mission leadership asking a question which many had already asked: "What are your plans for the future? Will you and the children return to the United States now?" I responded to these inquiries by saying that there were many things about the future still unknown to me. However, of two things I was certain.

First, I would return to the U.S. on furlough only after a substitute had been found to take my place at the school. I wrote in my prayer letter: "It will be difficult enough to carry on the work at Bethania without John. It would be almost impossible if I would leave, too. Someone must fill the gap. I do not want the Lord to say of me, *'I sought for a man among them, that should make up the hedge, and stand in the gap . . . but I found none.'*—Ezek. 22:30 (KJV)."

Herb and Sylvia Lange had been transferred to Emmaus High School in Koror in June of 1967, so we had no men missionaries left at Bethania. I knew that someone had to take up the slack. There was the new building to be completed; the boats to be supervised; the motors and machines to be cared for; purchasing to be done; the treasurer's job to be maintained; etc. All of this was in addition to the teaching responsibilities I had with Angela and in the high school. The most challenging aspect was—as an American woman I had to direct and pay the Palauan men workers. It was a frightening "mantle" which I had inherited and of which I knew I was not capable.

I prayed much for wisdom and strength, and took matters a day at a time. With my health somewhat uncertain, I knew that I should be resting more. Looking into the year ahead, it seemed most unlikely that I would have much rest.[1] But the Lord's promises were: "*'But I will restore you to health and heal your wounds,' declares the Lord*" (Jer. 30:17a) and "*As thy days, so shall thy strength be.*"—Deut. 33:25b (KJV).

Through the following nine months (prior to leaving Palau for my year of furlough) I found the Lord faithful as always to His promises. In spite of the many difficult problems and heavy responsibilities, my condition gradually improved. By the time I had returned to the States I was close to one hundred percent well again. In trying to analyze how I could possibly have made such an improvement under those conditions, I remembered the words of Nehemiah 8:10b: "*The joy of the Lord is your strength.*" Finding my joy and delight in doing the will of my Father had given me physical as well as spiritual strength.

My health was not, however, the main reason that I considered a furlough as soon as my replacement could be found. I had a burning desire to tell people across the U.S.A. about all the miracles of those six years. My heart cry was: "*That they may know that this is Thy hand; that Thou, Lord, hast done it.*"—Psa. 109:27 (KJV).

I had tried to keep the folks back home up-to-date on all that was happening, but I found it increasingly difficult to keep letters going out as often as I would have liked with my heavy schedule. A tone of desperation about the letter-writing problem can be detected in a prayer letter:

---

[1] See principle #14, Appendix.

Decisions, decisions . . .

It's 10:30 P.M. Shall I go to bed . . . or write letters?

It's Saturday. Shall I go witnessing to a village this weekend . . . or write letters?

The boat's leaving in two hours with the mail for Koror. Shall I teach Angela . . . or write letters?

It's Sunday afternoon. Shall I rest a while . . . or write letters?

The mail just came. Shall I read it . . . or write letters?

It's hard to choose. My physical weakness is ever present, and surrounding me are innumerable duties and responsibilities. We do praise the Lord for the many opportunities that He gives. He also gives the words to fit the opportunities, even to me. (Eight messages in one week over Christmas and New Year's, and a funeral message today without any notice!) How thankful I am that the Lord can use the poorest vessel that is dedicated to Him.

The varied aspects of missionary life are presented in excerpts from my prayer letter of April 1968:

Do you like to make picture puzzles? Ang and I made a beautiful one of David a few weeks ago. It's hard for you to get the real "picture" of missionary work in Palau from so far away. If I send you a few pieces, do you think you could fit them together to make a picture?

It was hard work, but our hearts were light as we unloaded $1000 worth of lumber and plywood from the boat for the women missionaries' residence in the new building. ($900 of paint is on its way from the U.S.) We had been waiting and praying for the materials to come to Koror by ship; for the money to come in so we could buy them; and for our boat to be repaired so they could be brought up to Bethania. Now the work can go on!

How easy it is to throw myself into the teaching of personal evangelism this semester. Now I know why it was John's favorite class. Remember these dear seniors, that the fire of Finney may kindle their souls!

Well, at last we caught the villain! He's been harassing us day and night for months. Angela finally lost her patience with him. Her wire trap baited with bread did the trick. She threw our dear "Friend Rat" into the water and drowned him. (She says she knows it was our "friend" because she recognized his face! I wonder how many relatives he has.)

It was the words: "The hours that I have wasted are so many; the hours I've spent for Christ so few" that touched Julia's heart. She came to the house in tears last Wednesday night after hymn-singing class. She wanted to pray about her wastefulness and the many lost souls back home in Kosrae. The Lord had spoken to her as we learned our new song: *"I Wonder, Have I Done My Best for Jesus?"*

The pieces don't fit together to make a clear picture? I'm sorry. If the Lord is willing, I may see you before 1968 is over, and maybe I can bring the picture to life. If you are interested in seeing the above picture in "living color," let me know.

Many other events of note happened during that first half of 1968, but two are never to be forgotten. The first is recounted in a letter written by Angela to children in the U.S.:

I would like to tell you about something that happened to me last week. My friend Alphonse and I made a little picture storybook with three children's gospel stories in it. Lisa and Sadaria (Palauan graduates from the Far Eastern Bible Institute and Seminary), Alphonse and I went up to a village in the mountains to visit the people there.

Lisa and Sadaria left us and went farther up to talk to the grown-ups. Alphonse and I gathered the children together to have Sunday School. She taught some songs and a Bible verse. There was one three-year-old boy who was very attentive. This boy was so interested while I taught the story that he stood up right in front of me. I told him to sit down, but he didn't take his eyes off the story until I finished. When we were finished, I gave all the children Sunday School papers.

When the boy went home, an old lady asked him where he had been. He said, "I was listening to the Pastor's daughter teach about Jesus and God." Holding up the Sunday School papers, he said, "These are God's letters to me. When I go home I'm going to tell my parents about Jesus."

The next day the little boy's mother told him to watch the baby while she went to wash the clothes in the river. She told him not to make any noise or the baby might wake up. She hung the rope for the swing up over the rafters so he couldn't swing and wake the baby.

When she left, he took the Sunday School papers and looked at them. Then he wanted to swing. He saw the swing was hanging down just far enough for him to put his chin over it. So he did. When his mother came back, there he was hanging by his chin—dead! What a sudden death!

I think this will bring his parents closer to the Lord. Will you pray for them?

Sandy was involved in the other event. I was really looking forward to seeing Sandy again. Since the Philippine school year ended about the middle of April, I had planned for Sandy to be with us in Palau for six weeks before we all left together on furlough. Since we had not seen each other since his father's death, I felt that it would be an important time for all of us.

I wanted to be sure that the authorities at Faith Academy would buy Sandy's ticket early because the flights from Manila to Guam were always fully booked early. I sent them the plane fare in January with instructions to buy his ticket right away.

I waited for word from the school or Sandy about what flight he would be on, but nothing came. I knew when the school term ended, so I figured out the flight he would probably be on and went to Koror to meet it. Herb Lange drove me to the airport.

I eagerly watched every passenger who disembarked till the very last one. Sandy didn't come! It was disappointing, but I did not feel what Herb felt. On the ride back he was silent for a while. Then he said, "It's not fair! You have shown such a wonderful spirit through all that has happened to you this past year. *This just isn't fair!*" I gently reminded him that God is always "fair," even when we can't understand what He is doing or why.[2]

I stayed in Koror to meet the next plane, but Sandy wasn't on that either. I decided then that I must get back to Ngaraard to teach my classes. I asked Herb to try to keep a lookout, somehow, to see if Sandy might come on another flight soon. The next trip of the speedboat returning from Koror brought me a telegram which had arrived there after I left for Ngaraard.

It read something like this: "My teachers sent me to the States. I will meet you here. Sandy."

I gasped, sat down, and took a deep breath. Sandy in the U.S.? Why?? Where??? This meant that he would not be returning to Palau, and all my plans for us were shattered. This meant I would not see him for another five long weeks! For a few moments the disappointment was almost overwhelming. Then I remembered what I had told the girls so often: "The Lord always knows what He is doing, and He does all things well!" I gave up my dream to the Lord and told Him that it was O.K.

Then I returned to all the needs at hand and threw myself into the work, saying to the Lord, "Thank You for taking care of Sandy. You know where he is and why he is there. In Your good time I will hear from him or from the school and find out the answers to these questions."

Three weeks went by, and there was no further word. One day as I was preparing some things for furlough, it suddenly hit me: "Ang and I will be leaving here in less than three weeks and I don't know where my son is! The United States is an

---

[2] See principle #15, Appendix.

awfully big country. How will I find him? I can't get any information from Faith because the teachers have left for the summer. If I don't hear something soon, I will be leaving Palau not knowing how to find my son!"

It was a horrible feeling! I think I would have gone mad if it had not been for the comforting presence of the Lord.

A day or two later I finally received a letter from Sandy. Somehow the school authorities had neglected to buy his ticket, and when they finally went to get it, there were no seats available on the flights to Guam. Since almost all the teachers were leaving Manila, they didn't want to leave Sandy there somewhere, so his counselor who was going to the U.S. on furlough decided to use the money I had sent for travel to Palau to buy a ticket to the West Coast—since he knew from Sandy that I would be going on furlough in June. The counselor had friends in California with whom he arranged to "park" Sandy for the month until my arrival in Los Angeles.

All of this made me pretty nervous when Angela and I boarded the plane in Guam in June. It was five hours late leaving Guam, and the possibility was great that we would miss our flight in Honolulu. If we missed that flight, I had no way to contact Sandy, since his hosts and he would already be around the L.A. area.

The Lord was gracious, and after a long run from one end of the Honolulu airport to the other (in new shoes, after not wearing shoes for six years!), we got on the last bus just as it was leaving to go out to our plane. And when we touched down, there was Sandy's smiling face waiting for us in the huge Los Angeles airport. It was "a sight for tear-filled eyes"! Once again the Lord had proven His faithfulness.[3]

---

[3] See principle #16, Appendix.

12

FACING FURLOUGH

"I will go before thee and make the crooked places straight [i.e., unwind the snarls]."—Isa. 45:2a (KJV)

*O*ur six-year term was quickly drawing to a close. The Lord had guided me safely through some very sticky problems toward the end of the building construction, and we were actually able to have the dedication of our new 30-by 100-foot two-story building a few days before Angela and I left Bethania for the United States.

Could we say, "We're going home"? Where was "home"? Angela asked me one day if we would go back to live at "our house" in Darlington, Indiana, on furlough. I suddenly realized that she didn't know it was not "our house"! "Ang, we don't *have* a house. The house we lived in at Darlington belongs to the church. It is used by whoever is the pastor of the church, so another pastor and his family live there now."

We had no "home" in which we could stay for the year. We would visit for periods of time with my generous relatives to whom I wrote:

I think I have the best family anywhere. . . . I can't find the words for it, but I trust that the Lord will help you understand what a great encouragement and blessing your letters have been to me. Now all your offers to help are arriving. I'm sure that eternity will reveal that we will share alike in any fruit that is borne as a result of my presence in Micronesia.

To my father, who had serious health problems, I explained:

> Your invitation to stay with you, Dad, is just like you. You surely know that I wish I could spend the whole year there. You could lie on the couch and I on the floor, and we could try to catch up on all the wonderful things we have learned from the Lord in the past six years. Well, of course, I can't do that. But I am determined to spend the first month with you.

I did not know that the precious periods of time I spent with my Dad during that furlough year would be my last opportunity to be with him while he was on this earth. But then there is still eternity ahead to "catch up"!

My brother and sister-in-law had very graciously offered to keep the children in their home in Amarillo, Texas, during the school year. This would enable me to do the deputation which I felt I must do, not just because of our support needs but primarily because the Lord had opened many doors for me to tell our story. I knew that I must call Christians in churches around the country to awaken and begin answering the Lord's call to join Him in His great rescue operation.

I had written about some of the questions furlough posed for Sandy and Angela:

> As you pray, please remember the adjustment for the children. In some ways, I think it will be a greater one than when we came out here. The children are both in a critical time of their lives (13 and 15). It is difficult at that age to be different, and whether they like it or not, they *are* different. Sandy, of course, has been in a school somewhat like those in the States, only completely on a Christian level. Angela has had nothing but school alone.

I knew that it would be difficult for Sandy and Angela to feel "at home" in Texas. Palau and the Philippines are hot and humid. The temperature never varies more than 10 or 15 degrees from the hottest to the not-quite-so-hot. Palau, particularly, is right at sea level. Life in Palau is generally slower and more relaxed. Food is very different from that in the U.S.

Clothes are not very important, and are often stained. Shoes are seldom if ever worn. Angela, especially, had been free for six years to play and work with her friends, to go swimming or shelling and generally set her own schedule except during school hours. Her life was much more Palauan than American in content, and she spoke Palauan most of the time—except in the house, where I tried to keep up her English.

On the other hand, Amarillo is on a high plateau 4000 feet in elevation. The humidity is very low. The temperature goes through extremes of 50 degrees in a twenty-four hour period at times. Life is busy and bustling. Texas food is greatly influenced by the Mexican heritage of that state. Clothes can be *very* important, especially to teenagers. Shoes *must* be worn! Life in Texas as elsewhere in the U.S.A. is fully scheduled, and people are expected to keep up with the schedule. And nobody knows Palauan! In fact, almost no one knows there *is* a Micronesia out in the vast Pacific.

My concern for the adjustment of the children was added to my qualms for myself. How could I face a year of traveling and speaking all over the U.S.A. alone? Life in Palau suddenly seemed sheltered and easy in comparison. I had never aspired to be a public speaker. I had laughed at our Professor of Homiletics at Providence Bible Institute when he said I should consider becoming a woman preacher!

Would I be able to face all those strangers? More importantly, would I be able to get across to them all that the Lord had laid on my heart? What about those crowded highways? I hadn't driven once in six years. And I didn't have a car! Where would I get one? And if I had a car, would I be able to drive thousands of miles from meeting to meeting—alone?

Answers to my concerns came from my father and the Lord. In response to my Dad's letter I wrote:

> Your offer of your new Toyota for my use is really fabulous, Dad, but I wonder if you know what "my use" may involve before the year is over. Please let me know if you really mean that I should use it for the year or just while I am in Connecticut. I realize perfectly that cars are

expensive and that use deteriorates them. If you honestly feel that you can afford to let me use it on deputation, please let me hasten to tell you what an answer to prayer your offer is.

My generous father really did lend me his car for the whole year! When I first got home, I was terrified of driving. My Dad's confidence in me, as he said, "Come on, you drive," helped to overcome my fears.

During that year of furlough I often thought of the promises the Lord had given me while still in Palau to quiet my qualms:

"You will be blessed in the city, and blessed in the country . . . you will be blessed when you come in and blessed when you go out."—Deut. 28:3, 6.

"The Lord replied, 'My Presence will go with you, and I will give you rest.'"—Exod. 33:14.

How literally the Lord fulfilled these promises! His presence was with me over the long stretches of freeways and through the traffic-choked cities. He was with me in every meeting, whether before a handful or thousands. And the most amazing fact of all was the *rest* that He gave. I found driving, speaking, visiting from home to home, all restful! For He was there![1]

I had asked people to pray Paul's prayer for me, and that, too, was fulfilled:

"Pray also for me, that whenever I open my mouth, words may be given me so that I will fearlessly make known the mystery of the gospel. . . . Pray that I may declare it fearlessly, as I should."—Eph. 6:19–20.

1968 was the year I turned forty. I wrote to my father:

You might be interested in reading the verse the Lord gave me for my fortieth year. *"Remember how the Lord your God led you all the way in the desert these forty years, to humble you and to test you in order to know what was in your heart, whether or not you would keep His commands."*—Deut. 8:2.

---

[1] See principle #17, Appendix.

I do pray that in "proving" me He finds complete commitment to Him. However many years I have left here, I want to spend every moment of every one for my Lord. Nothing else is even worth thinking about.

One question that I was asked repeatedly on furlough was the same one the Mission leaders had asked right after John was taken. "What are your plans for the future? After your furlough is over, then what?"

The Lord had answered this question for me that night in 1961. I had not gone to the field as the wife of a missionary only. The call was to me personally. There was one certainty that I had regarding the veiled future. I would serve my Lord in Micronesia as long as He would allow me to. I did not need to ask with Isaiah, "Lord, how long?" I knew in my heart that the answer would be the same to me as it was to him: "Until there's no one left to tell!"—Isa. 6:11.

Halfway through the furlough year I wrote to friends: "It has been a thrilling six months, but one place has never left our thoughts—MICRONESIA! We are all a little homesick for our beautiful island world and all our dear friends there."

Actually, we were more than "a little homesick." At times Angela was actually sick, partly due to the radical climatic changes but primarily due to the lonesomeness she felt concerning her friends and her island home. Sandy was going through his personal trauma as well. There were moments when I, too, was temporarily overcome with homesickness and loneliness.

The day I left Amarillo and the kids once again, I was suddenly overcome with sadness and loneliness. As I drove north toward Colorado, I had to keep wiping away the tears in order to see the road clearly. It was then that I composed a song in my mind which many Micronesians have come to love in the years since:

"I Cannot Face the Future Without Jesus"

Can you face the future without Jesus?
Can you walk that lonesome road alone?

Do you dare to meet the unknown morrow,
Without a Friend whom you can call your own?
Chorus:
I cannot face the future without Jesus.
I cannot walk this lonesome road alone.
I would not dare to meet the unknown morrow,
Without the Lord to keep me for His own.

In April, I wrote from New Jersey to friends:

Here I am—one year, 180 meetings and 20,000 miles later—and about to take off on the remaining two-thirds of my round-the-world trip. . . . Lord willing, on May 18th, Sandy and Angela will arrive in New York from Amarillo. That same evening, we three will board a Lufthansa jet for Germany. We are scheduled to arrive in Stuttgart the following day. From there we will drive to Bad Liebenzell, the town where our Mission headquarters is located.

The reason we're leaving the States a month early is that we need to be at Bad Liebenzell for the big conference held there each year around Pentecost Sunday (tent meetings with 8000 to 9000 attending). Pray that the Lord will use us then and as we travel and speak for two months.

From Germany we plan to go on to the Philippines. The children will be going to school at Faith Academy where Sandy went for three years before. Sandy will be a senior and Angela in eighth grade. They will need to be there for school opening on July 22.

Arriving August 4th in Palau, I found Wanda Aigner in the hospital after having stepped through the floor of our old house. This plunged me immediately into the directorship of the Vacation Bible School training. Following that came preparation for school opening, with 135 girls, as our responsibility and opportunity. *"We were pressed out of measure that . . . we should not trust in ourselves, but in God."*—2 Cor. 1:8–9 (KJV).

13

THE SACRIFICES OF THANKSGIVING

"And let them sacrifice the sacrifices of thanksgiving, and declare His works with rejoicing."—Psa. 107:22 (KJV)

*M*y second term in Palau began more or less like the first one ended, giving occasion for me to write a letter to friends and supporters about "the sacrifices of thanksgiving":

Have you ever had the unique experience of spending Thanksgiving afternoon fixing a generator? Well, our boatsman-mechanic had left at 5 A.M. to take the Emmaus boys on a two-day outing to the Rock Islands, and the generator wouldn't run! So I read the manual, got out the tools, and went to work. Thanks to the Lord's faithfulness, I emerged from the generator building a couple of hours later, drenched with sweat and oil, but successful!

Our day started with a Thanksgiving Service in the school. We had told the girls to prepare themselves for a "Share the Blessings" meeting. And they did! Their special numbers and testimonies lasted from 8:30 till 12:20! Our hearts were stirred by the sincere testimonies. Sitting there, I was reminded of all the prayers and work that had been invested in the lives of these girls. Some of those testifying had been our biggest problems last year. Three told how they had come from Catholic families to Bethania, hardly knowing why they came. God's ways are *"past finding out."*—Rom. 11:33b (KJV).

WALKING THE WAVES

In the middle of the afternoon the mail boat arrived. We had received no mail for a week and had not expected it for another week because "mail boat day" was Thanksgiving—a holiday! I was quite touched as I contemplated the Lord's tender compassion for His children. He knew what great joy that gift of mail would bring to girls and missionaries alike.

In the mail came another surprise. We had been planning our Thanksgiving dinner and party for the evening. No matter how we racked our brains for ideas, it seemed mighty poor. Have you ever tried planning a Thanksgiving dinner (for a large crowd) with very little meat and no sugar? (We had had no sugar for several weeks.) In the mail came a beautiful new Billy Graham film entitled "His Land." I had ordered it, but it arrived *six days early*. (And could be shown with a fixed generator!) So, though our dinner was not very exciting, we were able to have a happy party concluding with this heart-searching film.

Tying up His day with a golden bow, the Lord brought one of our new Chuukese girls to the office at the end of the party. "I thought I was a Christian," Wendyna said, "but I know now that something is missing. Will you tell me how to really believe, Mrs. Simpson?" No matter how many times I do it, it's always a special thrill to lead someone into the presence of Christ and to see the joy of Jesus reflected on a face.

Standing alone in the darkness that night, waiting for the generator motor to run a while before shutting it off, I marveled at the work of our Lord. I thought again about my message in the morning around the words of the Psalmist in Psalm 107:22 (KJV): *"And let them sacrifice the sacrifices of thanksgiving, and declare His works with rejoicing."* Sometimes it is a sacrifice to be thankful. It's hard to be thankful that you don't have a very good Thanksgiving dinner, or that the generator breaks down. But when we are able to *"in everything give thanks"* (1 Thess. 5:18a, KJV), we can declare all His works with rejoicing.

THE SACRIFICES OF THANKSGIVING

Then what fountains of joy spring up from within to quench the thirsty soul and water the dry ground in every direction!

In that letter to friends I didn't mention the more serious problem that was looming ahead for me. I wrote to my father and stepmother about it on November 29th:

> I just returned from seeing the Peace Corps doctor in Koror. . . . There is no way of knowing whether the growth on my ovary is fibroid or cancerous without an abdominal hysterectomy. Since I was quite sick last week, and have been weak and weary for two months now, it seems imperative that it be taken care of soon.
>
> The doctor suggests that I have the operation at the Koror Hospital since he feels that they will be unwilling to admit me at the Naval Hospital in Guam. Sometime soon I think they will operate. If they find anything worse than a small amount of cancer, they will sew me up again and fly me out to the Naval Hospital, in which case they would be obliged to admit me as a patient.
>
> My heart is perfectly at rest in the Lord. I trust that whatever the outcome may be, He will be glorified.

I did not tell my parents that the Palauan doctors who would operate were only medical orderlies, and that the conditions in the Koror Hospital were not quite "ideal."

I also did not write to them about the struggle I had had in dealing with this life-and-death issue facing my children and me. When I went to the Lord with it, He comforted and strengthened me from His Word, as always. He again used Psalm 31:19–24: *"How great is Your goodness, which You have stored up for those who fear You. . . . In the shelter of Your presence You hide them. . . . Praise be to the Lord, for He showed His wonderful love to me when I was in a besieged city. . . . In my alarm I said, 'I am cut off from Your sight!' Yet You heard my cry for mercy when I called to You for help. . . . Be strong and take heart, all you who hope in the Lord."*

I am glad that I had learned about the "sacrifices of thanksgiving" before I had to meet that next challenge. It's not easy to spend your Christmas 1500 miles from your children, and 9000 miles from the rest of your family, very sick and in pain. Hospital rooms can be lonely places, especially in a foreign country at a time of the year when those who are your friends in the area are very busy. The Lord came through for me as He always has! I expressed my feelings in a letter to friends and family written on Christmas Day, 1969, from the Koror Hospital.

Have you ever spent Christmas in the hospital? If you ever do, I trust you will find it as I have—*a most unusual experience*!

Enclosed now for a week in my little 8- by 8-foot postoperative cubicle with no window to the outside world, I have come to recognize it as the "wilderness" of which the Lord spoke to me in Hosea 2:14: *"Therefore, behold, I will allure her and bring her into the wilderness, and speak comfortably to her heart."* [1] Here, in my "wilderness," the Lord and I have spent precious, uninterrupted hours together and He has spoken to my heart, as I have had a Christmas gift which you perhaps did *not* receive—*time to listen!* [2]

I've had *time* to be thankful for little things. What a fountain of gratitude bubbled up in my soul for a wet cloth on a perspiring forehead; those early shots bringing relief from pain and restful sleep; that faithfully whirring fan in the corner, without which the room would be insufferable; that mouthful of liquid which finally went down and didn't want to come back up; that first painful, but successful, attempt to walk alone.

I've had *time* to appreciate the kindness of others. In this little, understaffed hospital with only partially trained personnel, I have noted with gratitude that the doctors and nurses have tried to take care of me according to their understanding of "American standards." I have been

---

[1] KJV marginal reading.
[2] See principle #18, Appendix.

moved as fellow missionaries, at this busiest season of the year for them, have taken some of their precious time to check on my progress, bring me a bowl of hot soup, or sit down for a while to chat and pray.

I'll bet that you didn't read all of the verses on all of your Christmas cards. Well, I did! Because I had *time*! Your notes and letters have been like *"waters in the wilderness and rivers in the desert"* (Isa. 43:20b, KJV) as you have encouraged me with your love. Tears of deepest thanksgiving overflowed as I read about plans for the children's happy Christmas activities. They are spending Christmas vacation together with the family of their much-admired music teacher. I was quite touched by a letter from one of our dear Palauan girls at FEBIAS in which she mentioned how Sandy had sung a solo on a recent Sunday morning in the Capitol City Baptist Church in Manila. May the Lord "make him a blessing," like he sang. Ang was obviously elated over the success of their school Christmas operetta, in which she had the part of the Christmas Spirit. "I guess my solo was O.K.," she wrote, "because Sandy even kissed me on the forehead afterward."

So this has been my Christmas. It's true there were no silver bells, or snow-covered lanes. In fact, there were no colored lights or Christmas trees or gaily wrapped presents. The family was not gathered around for feasts and parties. But Jesus and I have had our simple Christmas together and I think I shall remember it longer than any other.

I added a postscript to my letter for those who had not heard the reason for my hospital visit:

I began to experience symptoms in September which led to the discovery of a growth on my left ovary. After tests, x-rays and examinations, the doctors decided on an abdominal operation a week ago today. They found both ovaries covered with cysts. They removed the ovaries, tubes and appendix and cut out some attached cysts.

Although they did not appear cancerous, the report of the biopsy will be back next week.

I waited for a month, but received no report of the biopsy. I finally went down to the hospital. When I talked to the Palauan woman who had performed the operation, I discovered that the nurse had made an error. Instead of sending the growths away to be checked, she had sent the appendix to Hawaii and thrown the growths in the trash! So we had no way of finding out whether there was any malignancy. The following summer when I was checked in Guam, however, no irregularities were discovered.

I found the Lord to be very personal, loving and protective as I had to meet all the challenges of life as a widow, alien, teacher, treasurer, village missionary and general "handy-man." Again and again He has reminded me through the years of His care, speaking to me from Isaiah chapter 54:

"Do not be afraid; you will not suffer shame. Do not fear disgrace; you will not be humiliated. You will forget the shame of your youth and remember no more the reproach of your widowhood.

"For your Maker is your husband—the Lord Almighty is His name—the Holy One of Israel is your redeemer; He is called the God of all the earth.

"The Lord will call you back as if you were a wife deserted and distressed in spirit. . . . For a brief moment I abandoned you, but with deep compassion I will bring you back. . . .

"Though the mountains be shaken and the hills be removed, yet My unfailing love for you will not be shaken nor My covenant of peace be removed," says the Lord who has compassion on you. . . .

"If anyone does attack you, it will not be My doing; whoever attacks you will surrender to you. . . . No weapon forged against you will prevail, and you will refute every tongue that accuses you."

While I was surrounded daily by a multitude of needs and responsibilities, my thoughts and prayers were often with my distant children who were dealing with the problems and anxieties of the teen years. I expressed my concerns to my father, my most faithful prayer supporter, in 1970, three months before Sandy's graduation from Faith Academy:

> Please pray for my children—that the Lord will mercifully use what we have tried to do to lead them close to Him, and that they will be able to forget all our mistakes and failures. Pray that the Lord will help them to understand and accept joyfully all the things which make their lives so different from the lives of most young people. I wonder how Isaac felt that day when his father tied him up, put him on the altar, and raised the knife to kill him. Do you suppose he understood that his father loved him more than anyone but *God*? Well, at least he understands now.

I was aware that my father was in daily prayer for us, and I felt that he understood the physical and spiritual battles we were going through better than anyone else. When my dear Dad became terminally ill with cancer during that term of mine on the field, I could not go to see him. When he died, I felt a severe loss, not so much of his presence as of his prayers.

•   •   •

In the couple of years that followed, Sandy entered into a dark valley that cast its shadow over Angela and me as well. For over two years I wept and prayed for my son, whom I knew was wandering. I did not feel that I could share this burden with anyone because of my fear that general knowledge of it would damage Sandy's reputation and cause him even further discouragement. I clung tenaciously to the Lord only, reminding Him often of His promise: *"All thy children shall be taught of the Lord; and great shall be the peace of thy children."*—Isa. 54:13 (KJV).

Frequently I reread the verses I felt the Lord had showed me about Sandy years before. It was as if I could hear Sandy speaking: *"Listen, O isles, unto me; and hearken, ye people, from far; the Lord hath called me from the womb; from the bowels of my mother He hath made mention of my name. And He hath made my mouth like a sharp sword; in the shadow of His hand hath He hid me, and made me a polished shaft; in His quiver He hath hid me; and said unto me, 'Thou art my servant . . . in whom I will be glorified'"*—Isa. 49:1–3 (KJV). But how could such things be fulfilled in Sandy when his heart was hardened toward God and his life a mess?

Some days I was almost overwhelmed by the hopelessness of the situation. Then it was that the enemy tried his best to make me doubt the words of my Lord. I was determined to cling to the promises of the God of the impossible, remembering that He had often raised dead hopes and dead people. And the Father continued to encourage me with His promises in the darkness: *"I will raise him up in My righteousness. I will make all his ways straight. He will rebuild My city and set My captives free."*—Isa. 45:13a.

I spent many hours on my knees in tears, pleading with the Lord to do the miracle of bringing back my son to Himself. One night I read a small pamphlet that explained a bit about spiritual warfare and the importance of taking a definite stand against the evil spirits of which we become aware. I was convinced that night that there were evil spirits at work in Sandy's life. I decided to take the stand of Ephesians 6. In the all-powerful name and authority of Jesus the Lord, I bound the demons who were harassing Sandy and commanded them to stop. A week or so later I received a letter from Sandy, saying that he knew he must get right with God. He asked, "Could I come to be with you for a while?"

I prefer to have Sandy tell the story in his own words. In 1992 he put out a solo album entitled *"Back Over the Waves."*[3] The insert in the album is a detailed testimony, from which I take the following:

> They say missionary kids are the children most likely to secede. There are many pressures associated with growing up on the mission field. In my case, being sent

---

[3] Alexander J. Simpson, Album: *"Back Over the Waves"*; Agana, Guam, Outrigger Productions, 1992.

away to school by myself to the Philippines at the tender age of 12, having to grow up away from my Palauan homeland, and having my father die in a boating accident during my finals week at Faith Academy didn't help to reduce my adolescent stress factor. But I learned later that these things were merely symptoms, branches on a tree that was rooted in rebellion.

Even though I had heard practically every sermon, Bible verse and hymn by the time I was in high school, I found my heart growing ever colder toward the gospel. By the time I was halfway through college, I was already doubting the very existence of God. I began to experiment with drugs, alcohol, social behaviors, and even the occult, to try to find the answers I was running away from.

I had been attending a college in the States, but decided to move out to Guam in 1972 to attend college there and to be closer to home. I was studying acting and music for a while, but soon I felt my education was lacking somehow. I found myself doing things like taking LSD right before I went on stage to star in a play; taking horse tranquilizers and attempting to write "inspired music"; or snorting cocaine and recording an all-night jam session.

I let myself go way out on a limb with the rest of my friends who were supposedly "searching." But I couldn't find any answers. I began to question everything. I was like a man who put a message in a bottle and was waiting for someone to find it and send back some kind of response. Anything! But, as I stood on the shore, I saw nothing but my face staring back at me in the ocean of my rebellion. I was profoundly and terribly alone.

Yes, believe it or not, the story does get bleaker. It all seems so far away now, but as I write this down, I am reminded vividly of how I felt. I met some ex-Warner Brothers executives who had moved to Guam to escape the "L.A. rat race." We bought a coffeehouse in Merizo, Guam, and had the use of a 52-foot catamaran on which we would take tourists around Cocos Island and sing and play for them. I thought I had it made.

Then some unusual things started to happen. I began to notice that if, when we played a concert, the wife of our band leader was present, our little trio of two guitars, a flute and vocals took on the sound of many more musicians than were present. This culminated in a concert we did in the largest movie theatre on Guam in front of about a thousand people. The point is, they all heard it too! Things would get lost and magically reappear. The group members taught me a certain kind of whistle and told me to use it if I needed to be picked up for practice. (At that time I lived on the other side of Guam and did not have a car.) One day I couldn't get a ride and decided to try it out. Within minutes they were outside my door. They said they had heard me whistle.

One night, in my usual drug-blind stupor, I had a dream. At least that is what we will call it here. A dark figure came to me and offered me power over all those people in Merizo, with only one condition—that I unequivocally and finally renounce any remaining belief I had in God. I told that dark demon to go away but I would think about what he had said. Next morning, I found myself lying in a ditch somewhere in Sinayana. People were passing by on the road but no one was stopping to help me. I knew I had to make a decision. I knew my mother was praying for me. I decided to tell my friends I was leaving Guam. Then the storm began.

They made it very hard for me to leave. They threw temptations in my path like bones to a hungry dog. And still, my mother prayed on. It amazes me that, even though she knew about many of the things I was going through, she never wrote me off in her life or in her letters to me. She would merely say, "I love you, Jesus loves you, and I'm praying for you." This had a profound effect on what rebellious spirit I still had left after all my self-destruction. Today I look back and see what a diffi-

WELCOME TO MICRONESIA:

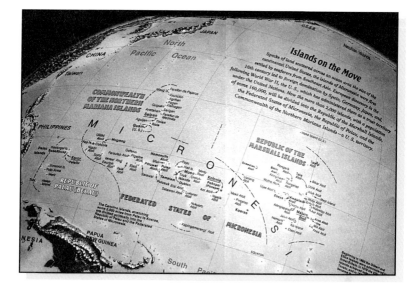

Micronesia spans 3000 miles of the Pacific.

Our big day! June 5, 1948 at Clinton, Connecticut.

John, a dynamic preacher! At the Congregational Christian Church, Darlington, Indiana.

The United States headquarters of Liebenzell Mission, Schooley's Mountain, New Jersey. Besides offices, this building serves as a guest house, with chapel, dining room and several meeting rooms.

We four at sea, on our way to Palau.

Our tropical paradise.

Island-style fun.

Angela and "sechelil"
(her friends).

Bethania girls dressed in
"uniforms" and leis.

Palauan "bai"
(community house).

Beach picnic.
In just a minute Mary will have
your "plate" ready.

The fishermen return.

There's nothing like a coconut to quench your thirst on a hot day.

Bethania High School campus.

"Hurry up! The bell rang for class!"

*"The Chorrekim's here.
Let's unload!"*

*John preaching at a
Deacon's Conference
in a bai (community house).*

*Ministry to Ngetbang,
an unreached village:
John with the
village chief and
Pastor Chelechuus.*

Memorial at Bethania campus.

Angela at Faith Academy in the Philippines with Palauan friends.

Sandy with his ever-present guitar.

Aftermath of a typhoon.

Bethania life goes on: buying produce for the school kitchen from a local farmer.

Graduation at last.

Three generations waiting for our little plane at the Angaur "terminal."

Ministry Through Micronesia:

A workshop in Chuuk.

The church in Maap, Yap.

A Bible study in Yap.

My plane at Ailinglaplap, Marshall Islands.

Fully decorated after an alumni party in Ebeye, Marshall Islands.

The alumni choir sang and I preached in Majuro, Marshall Islands.

Prison ministry on Guam, with friends.

Juanita Simpson

SIMPSON FAMILY PORTRAIT

Standing, left to right: *Steve, Angela, Kurtis & Jessica Leuice, Rose & Sandy Simpson.*
Seated, left to right: *Ashley & Kristin Leuice, Josiah Simpson, "Mamang" (that's me), Carissa & Cassie Simpson.*

cult time this must have been for her . . . there she was, a well-known missionary in Palau, and here I was, a well-known drug addict on Guam. Through her prayers and the prayers of others, I was finally able to step on that plane for home. I felt a great burden lift off me. The demons of Guam no longer had a hold on me. I bowed my head and accepted the Lord Jesus back into my heart, just as I had when I was only six years old in my father's church back in Indiana.

I was now back in Jesus' arms, but much of my ability to think and talk had been eroded away by long years of drug abuse. After many nights of tears, I resolved myself to the fate I knew I had inflicted upon myself. And I felt that it was a just punishment for me to live in a fog for the rest of my life. I was simply happy that Jesus had saved me. But then an amazing thing began to happen. My mind began to heal! Four years later God had given me a free gift that I did not deserve.

Sometime later, as I reflected back over those sad, painful months of agonized waiting on God to bring Sandy back to Him, I recalled the experience of twelve years earlier. I remembered the weeping and soul-searching I had done in our parsonage in Indiana when the Lord had reminded me of the faith of Abraham lived out in the attempted sacrifice of his only son Isaac. It was then that I had placed my children forever in the Lord's hands.

Somehow in my pain I had forgotten the verses the Lord had showed me at that time from Hebrews 11: *"By faith Abraham, when he was tried, offered up Isaac; and he that had received the promises offered up his only begotten son, of whom it was said, 'That in Isaac shall thy seed be called'; accounting that **God was able to raise him up, even from the dead,** from whence also he received him in a figure"* (vs. 17–19). How I rejoiced in the great God of Abraham who had once again proved His faithfulness by raising up my son "from the dead"!

14

DEFENDER OF THE FATHERLESS

"He defends the cause of the fatherless and the widow, and loves the alien, giving him food and clothing."—Deut. 10:18

J never told my children what my prayers for them were. I wanted so much for them to feel free to walk with God and follow His leadership wherever He might call them. But I have to confess that from the time they were small, I prayed that they would both be missionaries. And sometimes I felt guilty. Was I trying to control their lives through prayer? God knows that my motives were pure. Because I believe in my heart of hearts that the greatest calling on this earth is to serve the Lord as a missionary, I was only asking the best for my children. I was also painfully aware that parents sacrifice a great deal when their children go to a foreign country, requiring years of separation. What I requested of the Lord had the potential of bringing me much pain.

As my children grew, the Lord began giving me promises about Sandy and Angela that convinced me that my heart's desire for them was also His heart's desire. I have come to believe that when we are in tune with God, the Holy Spirit whispers God's thoughts into our minds. Thinking they are our desires, we begin to ask God for them. He, in turn, is delighted to give us our requests which came from Him in the first place. *"Delight yourself in the Lord and He will give you the desires of your heart."*—Psa 37:4. What a blessed partnership it is between mere mortals and the immortal *"God of all the earth"*! —Isa. 54:5.

WALKING THE WAVES

The Lord showed me that my children would indeed be missionaries: *"Know for certain that your descendants will be strangers in a country not their own."*—Gen. 15:13a.

I wondered how this could be possible for Sandy after the serious problems he had experienced. I thought perhaps the Lord was speaking of those other "descendants" I have in Micronesia—my spiritual sons and daughters. From the same chapter in Genesis, the Lord showed me that He was referring to my natural children: *". . . a son coming from your own body will be your heir."*—Gen. 15:4b.

The Father also assured me that He would be responsible to prepare and bless Sandy and Angela so that they would be equipped to serve Him: *"I will pour out My Spirit on your offspring, and My blessing on your descendants."*—Isa. 44:3b. *"The fruit of your womb will be blessed."*—Deut. 28:4a. I knew that our Father could be trusted to care for us because He had reminded me again and again in Scripture of His personal care for widows and the fatherless.

I never asked the Lord to send my children as missionaries to Micronesia. I did not know where He might want them to serve, until He showed me: *"And I will give unto thee, and to thy seed after thee, the land wherein thou art a stranger . . . for an everlasting possession; and I will be their God."*—Gen. 17:8 (KJV).

From Isaiah 49 I understood that my children would gather where I was, as if requesting space to live in. When that happened I would be amazed and say in my heart, *"I was alone, bereaved and barren. But these—where have they come from?"* (vs. 18–21). It was hard to be alone. Some days I felt so lonely for my children. For years they were thousands of miles away in high school or college, and I saw them at most for three months in the summer. Many years I didn't see them at all. I recognized from God's Word that this was evidently His choice for me as it was for Abraham: *"I called him alone, and blessed him and increased him."*—Isa. 51:2b (KJV).

Was the Lord now saying that He would increase and bless me sometime in the future by calling Sandy and Angela to serve in the islands we all loved? It seemed too good to be true. Maybe I had misread what the Lord wanted to communicate to me! I kept these words in my heart, waiting for the day when God might fulfill them, but I mentioned them to no one. My children will hear of them for the first time when they read this.[1]

Sandy was still with me, recuperating in Palau in April of 1974. The Lord generously supplied us with the funds to be able to go together to the Philippines to attend Angela's graduation from Faith Academy. How proud I was of my beautiful, talented daughter, and how grateful for my son who had been rescued and was in the process of healing.

After graduation we went to the "four winds" again. Angela took off from Manila for Europe, as she was privileged to sing with the Madri-Gals and Guys on tour in Europe and in the eastern United States. Sandy left Manila for Oregon, where he planned to settle for a while. I returned to Palau to finish the school year. It was the fifth year of my second term, so I was due to leave on furlough in June. The plan was for me to fly to Portland to meet Sandy; then we would go on together to meet Angela in Chicago at the end of the tour. Our summer would be spent visiting friends and relatives on the East Coast and then, across country, back to Oregon where Angela would attend college.

Anticipating Angela's college years, I had been quite concerned. It seemed to be such a difficult and dangerous situation for her to be alone in the great United States with me 9000 miles away and no family nearby to help her. I was not worried about Angela's character or goals. I knew that she was headed in the right direction. In her freshman year at Faith the Lord had done a special work in her during a revival at the school. It had resulted in her recommitment to missions. Now her only desire was to prepare herself. She told her friends at Faith that she would probably be a single missionary to Russia.

I felt good about the confidence I had in Angela's relationship to the Lord. But I had no such confidence in the young

---

[1] See principle #19, Appendix.

men whom she would be meeting! Being a very pretty girl, she often attracted stares on the street. Would she be safe?

All of my anxieties, of course, I took to our Father in prayer. I began asking the Lord to give Angela a godly boyfriend soon after arrival in the U.S., so that she would have his protection. I also asked for a family who would be close and would care enough for her to help her in times of need.

I really enjoy giving glory to God by telling the story of how He answered. Shortly before I left Palau to head for Portland and then Chicago, I received a letter from Ang written from Buffalo, New York. In it she wrote, "Mother, I think I have met the man I am going to marry!" I was relieved that I would soon see her, to be able to ask the details!

The story went like this: The first church on the East Coast where the Madri-Gals and Guys sang was the large and well-known Brookdale Baptist Church in Bloomfield, New Jersey. That night as Angela stood in the center of the choir singing, a dark-haired young man sat in the front row with his eyes fixed on her. Following the concert, the young man approached Ang, asking her to go out with him. She turned him down, not bothering to explain to him that they were not supposed to have dates on their tight concert schedule.

Steven Leuice went away disappointed, not knowing that Angela was as attracted to him as he was to her. She was able to get his address from one of the young people, and when the choir left the next day she began corresponding with him. Much to her surprise, Angela found herself becoming more and more interested in Steve.

The day came, while the choir was in Buffalo, that Angela decided she must give Steve a call. She felt herself falling deeply in love and she was worried about it. Her commitment to the Lord to be a missionary could be in jeopardy if Steve was going a different direction. She had better find out quickly, and call the whole thing off if necessary!

Angela's friends huddled around the phone. What would Steve's answer be? When Angela asked him what his plans were, Steve explained that he had planned to become a veterinarian. However, a few months previous, there had been a missions conference at the church and Steve had gone forward to indicate his willingness to serve the Lord on the mission field. He would begin his preparation in the fall at Northeastern Bible College.

Angela and her friends rejoiced together, after which she wrote to me that she had probably met the man she would marry. When I spent time with Steve that summer I was so grateful for God's excellent choice of a boyfriend for Ang! And I soon found that Steve's family were the kind of helpful, generous people that she so much needed. The Lord had answered my prayers, as He so often does, with great creativity and generosity. *"Now to Him who is able to do immeasurably more than all we ask or imagine, according to His power that is at work within us, to **Him** be glory."*—Eph. 3:20–21a.

During the Christmas vacation, Steve came to Newberg, Oregon, where we were spending the holidays together. I enjoyed getting to know him better. By the end of that vacation I had agreed to allow Angela to transfer to Northeastern Bible College, where she would be able to study more of the subjects she felt she needed for missionary preparation and be close to Steve.

Angela's college years were not all "wine and roses." She struggled with homesickness for the islands, a poor self-image, and financial constraints. But at least she was not alone! The Lord Himself was her Defender, and He provided others to help her as well.

•   •   •

With my return to Bethania, life in the islands continued on about the same—with lots of problems, overwhelming needs, and much schooling by the Lord. Occasionally we were taught huge and startling lessons. My prayer letter of April 1976 describes one such "class":

It had been very hot and dry for a week or more. The water level in our little reservoir had dropped very low. We decided to have only morning and evening water hours, and began to pray for rain. God answered *in abundance* the following day, April 7th!

It had rained most of the night. In the morning it was raining so hard and the gusts were so strong that we debated about whether we should have classes. After we had decided to try until chapel time, the local sanitarian came to report that the radio was announcing that Palau was in "typhoon condition two."

During my home economics class we looked out to see our speedboat about to sink. The seniors and I dropped our books and ran out in the driving rain to drag the boat to safety on the shore. At chapel time we canceled classes for the rest of the day, after my brief message from Psalm 148:8: *"Stormy wind fulfilling His word. . . ."* I pointed out that the wind goes where the Lord sends it, and sometimes He sends it to show us our weakness so that we will learn to trust only His strength.

The wind velocity kept rising, and by evening when I was showing some filmstrips to the seniors it was hard to hear above the howling wind. Suddenly there was a great crash and the lights went out. After finding my flashlight, I forced open the door, which was difficult because of the force of the wind and rain against it. There lay the whole 100-foot length of school verandah roof and the electric wires with it. It had landed on the walkway directly in front of our door. I peered anxiously into the darkness for signs of a head, leg or arm! With a sigh of relief and prayer of thanks, I saw that no one was pinned under it.

With the protection of the roof gone from the verandah, now our living room, the principal's office, the tenth and eleventh grade classrooms and home economics room were inundated with rain driven by the wind. I went out to move whatever I could in an attempt to keep sewing machines, books, etc., relatively dry.

Later in the evening three of the teachers came over. They had decided to stay with us since their house is old and shaky. We were making up their beds when we all heard a horrendous tearing of wood and roofing sheets. I ran into the dormitory. There lay the girls on their bunk beds looking up into the sky with the rain pouring down on them. Half the dormitory roof was gone!

Now it was *dangerous* to be in our building, to say nothing of WET! It was also dangerous to leave it! We gathered the girls and ran gingerly but hurriedly across the campus with our pillows and blankets to the other dorm. We arrived safely but soaked through.

Since we have no louvers on the new dorm windows, the rain was blowing all the way across the rooms. The girls had moved their beds to the side away from the wind, hung up sheets and bedspreads for protection, and were huddled together on the few partially dry beds. We joined them.

I don't think anyone slept much. Four or five in a single bed doesn't make for comfortable sleeping! We sang a lot of praise songs in many languages. We also did a lot of personal and joint praying as through the night we heard trees going down and roofs tearing up. Would our roof hold? It was still intact at 5:30 A.M. when we arose from our cramped quarters, praising God that everyone at Bethania was well and safe.

The dim morning light revealed a twisted mass of roofing sheets which had once been the other dorm roof. Seven other roofs were damaged, one half gone. Almost all the papaya and banana trees were down. Several of our precious kingkong (citrus fruit) trees were lost. One of the very tall coconut trees at the back had stood between the kitchen, dining room, food storeroom and pig pen. How we praised the Lord when we saw that it had fallen *opposite* the direction of the wind, missing all the buildings!

Running water greeted us as we went into our apartment! With no roof, a thin plywood ceiling doesn't hold back much water. It was running from all the ceilings, down the stairs, pouring through openings into the living room and kitchen. Our food cupboard looked like a waterfall was coursing over it. Many of our personal belongings were wet and a number ruined.

This morning (day after typhoon day) the Lord blessed my soul as I met Him in Psalm 46. I read: *"God is our refuge and strength, a very present help in trouble. Therefore will not we fear, though the earth be removed . . . though the waters roar and be troubled. . . . Come, behold the works of the Lord, what desolations He hath made in the earth. . . . Be still, and know that I am God."*—vs. 1–3, 8, 10 (KJV).

I shared these words from the Lord with the girls at chapel this morning. Amidst the debris, we sang and spoke about all the blessings we have to be thankful for. Then I read to them the special promise the Lord gave me this morning for our present and future needs. It is verse 5 of the same psalm: *"God is in the midst of her: she shall not be moved: God shall help her, and that right early"*![2] Praise the Lord with us for the speedy help He has promised!

Did the Lord keep His promise of speedy help? Everyone who has ever lived in Micronesia knows that not much of anything is done speedily in the islands! But our Lord is always true to His promises. I was able to report His faithfulness in letters written in July:

So many people gave so generously for "Bethania typhoon relief" that we could purchase many of the necessary materials quickly. Then the Lord saw to it that the new building materials had all left Guam before *their* devastating typhoon hit! Now I'm happy to report that most of the typhoon damage has been repaired.

The nicest assistance to arrive was Angela and her friend Steve, who came as summer missionaries to help us out. Their help, encouragement, and lively company was a real pleasure to me. They were kept busy doing assorted jobs: baking

---

[2] See principle #20, Appendix.

bread, making cement blocks, typing, making hoe handles, painting tanks, sewing clothes for me, taking charge of our summer youth meetings and preparing handcraft materials for Vacation Bible School. Our Palauan girls came to Bethania for a week, in which we teachers trained them. Following the training, the girls had eight Vacation Bible Schools with an approximate enrollment of 550.

A couple of months after Angela and Steve had returned to the States to attend their third year of Bible college, I received a cassette from them. I often exchanged news with my kids by way of cassette. On Sunday afternoons, if I was not in a village ministering, I would sit out on the beach and "talk" to them. Later they would "talk" back with the news of their busy lives.

This cassette was different. Steve asked me for my daughter's hand in marriage! They explained all their reasons for wishing to get married soon. I hastened to answer, giving them my blessing. Angela wrote in January, "Mom, Steve and I were engaged on Christmas Day! Isn't it exciting? We plan to be married early in the summer. Can you come? We really, really, really want you and Sandy to be here."

Once again my gracious heavenly Father, who loves to give His children good gifts, blessed me with a special trip to New Jersey to see my daughter and new son joined in marriage. Sandy was there, too, serving as "father," usher and soloist. He performed his original composition written for the occasion entitled *Only the Beginning.*

Ang and Steve continued striving toward their goal by writing to twenty-five missions for information. Meanwhile, they became more and more involved with the Liebenzell Mission, donating a considerable amount of their time to help with publications and printing. On advice from the Director, they decided to go to Wheaton Graduate School where they each worked toward a Master's degree in Cross-cultural Communications.

1978 saw Sandy returning to visit Palau after an absence of four years. In one of my letters I wrote:

He has been one of our workers for the past three months! He's busy every day with all kinds of jobs, including going fishing to supply the school with fish. (He caught a 42-pound tuna one day!) He has been a special blessing to the young people here and in Koror with his music and testimony. The young men of Palau are especially needy. Just a couple of weeks ago we were all shocked when our neighbor (who was Sandy's close friend when he was growing up) shot and killed a policeman in Ulimang (the village a half mile away). Part of the problem stemmed from the marijuana he has been growing and selling. This is being done throughout Palau these days.

Later Sandy wrote in the insert in his album *"Back Over the Waves"*[3] about how he felt about his life after four years of recuperation and restoration:

Those dark days of fighting, drinking and carousing had ill prepared me for the ministry God had told me I was supposed to have many years ago. I have to wonder now whether or not I am operating on "Plan B," but I suppose that is beside the point. At least I came around in the end. Now the question was, "How could I relate to all these nice folks who had never plumbed the depths like I had? How could a rough-hewn character like myself ever expect to minister to these gentle people?"

Like a close-up shot of a man sitting in the bleachers of a huge stadium full of people, the camera began to zoom out. I began to see a crowd of people whose souls looked remarkably like mine. There were people seated everywhere with troubled minds, shredded hearts, and broken spirits. Maybe the Lord was going to use me anyway. I could relate to these people!

Sandy's burden to help the island youth was growing. Some of the graduates of Bethania and Emmaus had the same burden. While my heart was full of rejoicing over the faithful

[3] Alexander J. Simpson, op. cit.

graduates of our Christian high schools in Palau, it was greatly saddened by reports from around Micronesia indicating the serious problems many of our graduates were encountering. I knew that in most places they had not received the spiritual support and encouragement they needed. I prayed long and with many tears, asking the Lord, "Who will help them?" I could hardly believe it when His answer came!

15

ENLARGING MY TENT

"Enlarge the place of your tent, stretch your tent curtains wide, do not hold back; lengthen your cords, strengthen your stakes. For you will spread out to the right and to the left; your descendants will dispossess nations and settle in their desolate cities."—Isa. 54:2–3

*J*t was Sunday morning. I was not in the chapel across the campus worshiping with the students and teachers; neither was I in Ngebuked at Arurang's house waiting to share with people coming from the village for our little Palauan worship service; nor was I in a boat heading for one of the other villages on Babeldaob, to minister there. I was lying on the bed in my room at Bethania. "Why am I feeling so lousy today, Lord? I never miss Sunday morning worship. Is there a reason why I am here by myself in this quiet place? Is there something special You want to say to me?"

Into my mind came an immediate answer: "I want to talk to you about your next ministry." *My next ministry?* I let that startling bit of information sink in for a minute or so. Then it dawned on me: so this is why the Lord has been gently weaning me away from Bethania![1]

Seventeen years of my life had been lived there on the east coast of the island of Babeldaob in the Palau chain. Bethania had been my home longer than any other home on this earth. I loved the Bethania High School! Every morning I could look out at the azure sea at our "doorstep." Every night I slept in my breezy room to the melody of the waves breaking on the reef. And the girls! True, they were sometimes dif-

---

[1] See principle #21, Appendix.

ficult and needed to be disciplined, but most of the time they were a delight to teach, to nurse, to play and work with, and to "mother."

Even when there were strenuous or stinky jobs to do, I could count on some of the girls to be right there to pitch in with me. Of course there were some lazy ones. But what about those who would get up out of a sound sleep when I called them late at night, telling them that the big boat had arrived and we needed to unload it before the tide went out? And what about those who would volunteer for the worst job on campus?

Waste from the girls' showers and toilets ran into a big septic tank in back, by the swamp. Every so often the tank would overflow and somebody had to dig big holes in other areas, scoop out the feces and deposit it in the holes. It was a dirty, smelly job that was extremely distasteful to everyone. Since I had a strong stomach, I always took the responsibility of working on this job. Not a single girl *wanted* to join me, but when I would ask for volunteers, fifteen or twenty hands would shoot up. They wouldn't dream of letting me struggle out there alone!

I had thought that I would probably live out the rest of my life on that tiny campus. I loved those girls as if they were my own daughters and I had no desire to leave. But several times in recent months the Lord had put into my mind a fleeting thought: "You will not always live at Bethania. You need to be prepared to leave when I tell you to."

So this was the time that the Father had chosen to reveal His plans for the future! "I want you to leave Bethania to travel around Micronesia, ministering to the graduates of Bethania and of Emmaus Boys' High School. You have been weeping and praying for them. Now go help them!"

Was my imagination overactive this Sunday morning? Or was this a real call from the Lord? My reaction was similar to the response I have often had when I felt that the Father was showing me something. "Lord, I believe this is Your call, but You know that I need confirmation from You. I cannot go ahead with a change of direction this drastic without absolute assurance from Your Word."

My Bible was open on my lap where I had been reading. I picked it up and read from First Peter. It sounded like something I would like to say to those alumni of the schools around Micronesia: "To *God's elect . . . scattered. . . . Grace and peace be yours in abundance. Praise be to the God and Father of our Lord Jesus Christ! In His great mercy He has given us new birth. . . . In this you greatly rejoice, though now for a little while you may have had to suffer grief. . . .*" As I read on, I could hear the Lord calling them to repentance and holiness, which I knew were two of their great needs.

Because the Father has so often given me direction from the book of Isaiah, I instinctively turned there. In chapter 58 I read about some of the spiritual responsibilities that the Lord wanted me to take for the needy graduates: "*. . . loose the chains of injustice . . . untie the cords of the yoke . . . set the oppressed free . . . break every yoke . . . share your food with the hungry . . . provide the wanderer with shelter . . . clothe the naked. . . .*"—Isa. 58:6–7. I knew that God was sending me to His children who were oppressed by the enemy, hungry for the Word, wandering, vulnerable and alone.

I have found in my life that the Lord never sends anyone to serve Him without providing all that he needs. As I read on, I found His personal promise of provision: "*If you spend yourself in behalf of the hungry and satisfy the needs of the oppressed, then your light will rise in the darkness, and your night will become like the noonday. The Lord will guide you always; He will satisfy your needs in a sun-scorched land and will strengthen your frame. You will be like a well-watered garden, like a spring whose waters never fail.*"—Isa. 58:10–11.

Continuing on in the same chapter, I was blessed to see that the Lord would use me and others to rebuild and repair the spiritual "ruins" in the islands: "*Your people will rebuild the ancient ruins and will raise up the age-old foundations; you will be called Repairer of Broken Walls, Restorer of Streets with Dwellings.*"—Isa. 58:12.

WALKING THE WAVES

The final biblical word of confirmation of God's call came that day from the chapter which the Lord had used again and again to direct, comfort and encourage me. I was to *"enlarge"* the place of my tent, *"stretch out," "lengthen"* and *"strengthen"* —Isa. 54:2. I smiled as I read that apt description of my earthly dwelling place: *"tent."* Sojourners live in tents, not permanent houses. Then I became very sober as I recognized God's warning and admonition in the middle of the verse: *"Do not hold back."* As always, I had a choice to make. I could hold back. I could refuse. I could deny that the Lord had spoken. [2]

My response to the Father was a humble commitment to follow His call, provided He went with me and empowered me to do His will. I reminded the Lord (as if He didn't know!) that I was under orders from the Liebenzell Mission and would not make any moves without the full agreement of the Liebenzell Director and Board. "I must also give the School Board of the Palauan Evangelical Church a year's notice so they can be looking for a new principal," I told my heavenly Father. Since I was just beginning the fifth and final year of my third term, I was due to go on furlough the following year. That would be a natural time for a change.

As I contemplated explaining all of this to our Director, Norman Dietsch, I knew that it must not be done through letters. I needed to see him face to face. But how? I asked the Lord to assure me that this was His will by sending Norman to Palau so that I could see him! It was an outlandish request, since Norman was only able to visit the islands every so many years, and usually for a very short period. Then I waited, not sharing this new development with anyone.

While waiting and praying about the new ministry, I heard from the Lord again. *"The Lord said to Abram after Lot had parted from him, 'Lift up your eyes from where you are and look north and south, east and west. All the land that you see I will give to you and your offspring forever. . . . Go, walk through the length and breadth of the land, for I am giving it to you.' So Abram moved his tents."*— Gen. 13:14–15, 17–18a.

---

[2] See principle #22, Appendix.

That summer we received word that our Director would be in Palau for several days, after which all of us Liebenzell missionaries would go with him to Yap for a missionary conference. I was awed at the workings of the Lord and prayed for the opportunity to speak privately to Norman.

When Norman arrived in Palau everyone wanted to see him. I arranged a private meeting with him three times, but each time someone else needed to talk to him, so I would acquiesce to them. I was getting nervous about when I could see him and what I would say when I did. The last night before we left Palau for Yap, the School Board of the Evangelical Church of Palau called a meeting with the two Directors who had come. Being principal of Bethania, I was a member of the Board, so I attended.

I sat next to Norman at the long table and listened while the Palauan Chairman of the Board asked a question of the Directors: "We would like to know what your opinion is of Bethania and Emmaus High Schools. Should we try to continue this program as it is? Should we change it in some ways? Do you think the schools have real value?"

Norman spoke up first. "The school program is excellent. I feel that there is a real value to it and that it is filling a need. However, it is not as effective as it might be because of the lack of follow-up. What is needed is a person who can travel throughout Micronesia, caring for the graduates and helping them in their present circumstances." Norman went on to describe in detail what he had in mind.

I could hardly contain myself! With a mighty effort, I forced back the smile that was coming to my lips and squelched the words that wanted to flow out. Norman was sitting there beside me, describing *exactly* the ministry to which the Lord had called *me*! But I had not said a word to him about God's call to this very ministry! All I could think was, "Lord, You are amazing! Now I know for sure that this is of You."

A few days later in Yap I finally was able to arrange a personal meeting with Norman. The Lord had already prepared the way for what I needed to say, so it was easy. I said, "Norman, remember what you said in the Palauan School Board meeting—about the need for someone to do follow-up with the Bethania and Emmaus graduates? Well, that's what the Lord has asked me to do on my next term!"

After listening to my complete explanation, Norman just said, "If that is God's call for your next term, then you need to consider the following on your furlough. . . ." How thankful I was to once again see how the God who calls also enables.[3]

To my supporters and friends I wrote:

Now as to my ministry when I return to Micronesia: For many years I have had a growing concern for all those who have attended Bethania and Emmaus and are now scattered throughout Micronesia (well over 1000!). As I have visited some at various times over the past years and been in correspondence with a number of them, I have heard them crying for help. They need counsel, encouragement, advice, teaching, materials for ministries, etc. The Lord has given me the privilege of knowing most of them personally. Now He is calling me to go where they are to minister to them any way I can on a personal basis.

God has begun a good work in these young people's lives. Many were born again while at the high schools here. A number grew to some spiritual maturity. But today as I look around Micronesia, I see a lot of "foundations" with no "houses" built on them. And yet other Micronesians are looking for the shelter and warmth they could experience if those "houses" were built. It is like an army badly needed for the warfare going on, but the soldiers are sick or asleep or they've misplaced their weapons.

I believe the Lord wants to reach Micronesians with Micronesians, but first they must be prepared. Lord willing, I will be traveling around the islands doing follow-

---

[3] See principle #23, Appendix.

up work to the good foundation already laid here in Palau. Exactly how this will be done, I do not know yet. With God's direction, your prayers, and good advice from all my Micronesian friends, I hope to be able to put together a realistic program of "helps."

•   •   •

Dramatic changes were taking place within the family as well. I described them in a letter to relatives and friends:

1980 promises to be an exciting, challenging, joyous, frightening, fantastically interesting and different year. The excitement started a few days ahead of time for our family with the birth of my first grandchild on December 27, 1979. Jessica Robin Leuice made a dramatic entrance into this world (by caesarean section) after all sorts of complications. Her mother, father and grandmother are all very thankful that she made it safely and at a hefty 8 pounds 11 ounces.

Ang and Steve are presently at the Liebenzell Mission headquarters going through their orientation as candidates. They hope to be coming out to Palau sometime within the next two or three months. This will begin a whole new challenging chapter in their lives. They will be involved in a new T.E.E. (Theological Education by Extension) program being started here. Their goal is to help in the strengthening of the church in Micronesia by teaching and encouraging the church leaders.

Sandy continues in his music, having concerts, writing commercials, and trying to work toward making a solo album. His exciting news these days has to do with his girlfriend, Rose. They sent me a neat tape last week. It was good to hear them tell about their activities and their relationship. They asked for prayers that they might be able to discern the Lord's will for their future.

How thankful I was that the Father had given Sandy a Christian girlfriend. How often I had prayed for her through the years without ever knowing her! A couple of months later,

I received the happy news from Sandy and Rose that they were engaged and planned to be married in June. They were asking for my furlough plans because they wanted to set the wedding date so that I could be there.

What a family reunion it was! In a letter full of pictures of the wedding, I tried to describe the details, but could not begin to express the emotions:

> June 17th was the BIG DAY!! It was my day to see my family again! You can imagine how often I had thought about it during the preceding months. It had seemed like a dream. The Lord in His kindness made this dream come true.
>
> I had come safely through the tension and trauma of leaving my dear home, Bethania, listening to and making many farewell speeches at all the parties, and finally waving good-bye to all the dear ones left behind in Palau.
>
> The following two weeks I had traveled through Micronesia, stopping to visit with Bethania and Emmaus grads, missionaries, and pastors in Guam, Chuuk, Pohnpei, Ebeye and Majuro. I had an exhaustingly wonderful time! At the same time I gained new vision and collected ideas regarding my ministry when I return to Micronesia after this furlough year.
>
> After stopping a few hours in Honolulu, I flew on to Portland, Oregon, a very excited mother (and grandmother and daughter). At the airport I was met by Sandy and his bride-to-be, Rose. What a thrill to meet my lovely almost-daughter-in-law!
>
> An hour later, we three met the jet arriving from New Jersey carrying Angela, Steve and Jessica—my new granddaughter. She is every bit as pretty and lovable as I had anticipated. It's fun to be a grandmother!
>
> We were still chattering away, trying to catch up on three years of news, as we walked to the other end of the terminal an hour later to meet *my* mother arriving from Florida. Four generations met for the first time!

We celebrated Ang and Steve's third anniversary on the 18th; Angela's 25th birthday on the 22nd; and finally, the big event, Sandy and Rose's wedding on the 28th. It was a lovely day and a beautiful wedding—and I am so very grateful to the Lord for giving my children such good Christian mates! Thank you for praying for them.

July 28th is our day to scatter again. Sandy and Rose will stay in Newberg, Oregon, where they live; Angela, Steve and Jessica will fly to Palau to begin their new ministry there; and I will go to the East Coast to begin my deputation.

That year of furlough was a busy one as always, as I crisscrossed the United States visiting churches and individuals. The Lord reconfirmed the call to the new ministry through many godly people. But the most important lessons I learned were lessons of faith. I needed those. He was helping me to "*stretch*" my tent curtains wide, "*lengthen*" my cords and "*strengthen*" my stakes, because that "*tent*" had become massive. It now had to cover three million square miles of ocean, and all the tiny dots of land sprinkled across it!

16

A HUGE FAMILY

"God sets the lonely in families, He leads forth the prisoners with singing; but the rebellious live in a sun-scorched land."—Psa. 68:6

*I*t was a darkness that could be felt! I couldn't see it but I could feel it descending like a great ominous cloud of doom. A voice which I couldn't hear with my ears spoke out of the cloud. It seemed to surround and smother me.

"Who do you think you are anyway, to be traveling around Micronesia? You are nothing but a little, weak woman. You can't help anyone! Besides, they don't even *want* you there! What will you do when you arrive at an island where nobody wants you? This is a stupid idea! You had better just go back to the United States where you belong and forget the whole thing!"

I was taken off guard. I quickly found myself agreeing with some of the statements made. I knew that I was a nobody—just a "little, weak woman." I was not at all sure that I would be able to really help Micronesians with all their problems. I definitely was uncertain about whether I was wanted or not. Of course, many of the graduates had told me when I had traveled through the islands earlier that they were waiting for me to come. But Micronesians are usually very polite and kind, and so would not want to offend me to my face. How did I know whether they meant it?

Up to a point I had to agree with my Accuser. But when it came to giving up what God had called me to, I was not so

WALKING THE WAVES

quick to acquiesce. Remembering Ephesians 6, I suddenly realized what I must do. I quickly reached for my *"shield of faith"* and *"sword of the Spirit."*

Directly addressing that accusing dark angel, I said, "Look at these verses! God called me through these verses and He gave me these promises. I have complete faith in my great Lord. He will go before me as He promised. He will help me to know what to do. He will empower me for this ministry to which He has called me. And even if nobody wants me, I know I will be doing my Father's will. And He will never leave me or forsake me. Now get out of here and don't come back!" The cloud lifted. Now I understood how important the new ministry must be for the enemy to go to such lengths to try to stop me![1]

I was in Palau. It was August of 1981. I was spending a month in prayer and preparation for my first trip around Micronesia in my new role. It was good to be able to stay with Steve and Angela, who were stationed in Koror. What a joy to be with them and my dear little granddaughter again!

My concern was to develop a ministry to the graduates according to their felt needs. I had written a letter to the alumni for whom I had addresses before I left the States, asking them two questions:

1. What are your greatest needs as a Bethania or Emmaus graduate?
2. In what ways do you feel I can help with those needs?

In the letter I gave my flight schedule. On my first exploratory trip I would spend about a week in each of the areas. I felt it was very important for me to meet with the church leaders so that I could explain personally what I planned to do and why. I needed their advice, and I also wanted them to be acquainted with me so that they would not wonder what this woman was doing in their islands!

I was anxious for the Micronesians to feel from the start that this was their "project." I did not want to arrive on their

---

[1] See principle #24, Appendix.

island with my plans all made and then just load them off on their shoulders. For that reason, I did not set up any dates for meetings or workshops before arriving in an area. I waited until I got there; then we would agree on what they wanted, as well as suitable dates and places.

I was determined not to travel through as a tourist. In some areas I could stay with the missionaries or in a Mission-provided room or apartment. In others there was no place like that in which to stay. I wanted the graduates to take as much responsibility as they could. So, as far as they were able, I expected them to care for me—providing meals and a place to stay. Where this was not feasible, I provided for myself. This plan resulted in my being able to spend a lot of time with individuals—at meals, and staying in their homes. And it gave the Micronesians a chance to help me as I was helping them. That was important for their self-esteem.

Following that first trip, I wrote to friends and supporters:

> Sometimes my spirit has grown faint during these past three and a half months as I have traveled from is-land to island. The needs are so great everywhere. My heart cries out to God as I see so many broken homes and broken lives. And I wonder how much I can really do to help. I know I cannot do much, but the Lord keeps urging me on, assuring me that He can mend, forgive, restore, and bring life out of death.

> On each island I have been trying to gather together as many of the graduates of Bethania and Emmaus as I can find. Some have been surprised to see me appearing at their offices or in their tiny villages. . . . Often we have presented a program of songs and a message in the church, or to the youth or the women. God has been good in helping me to make contacts with pastors and church leaders in each location. They have been open to my vis-its and some are asking me to help in their church pro-gram the next time I am there.

From this first exploratory trip I returned to Palau to begin preparation for the next year's ministry. I had decided to go around Micronesia once each year, spending anywhere from two weeks to four months in one location, depending on the number of alumni there and the opportunities for ministry that had been offered to me by church leaders. In short breaks between trips, I ordered materials for Sunday School teachers on each island. I also sent out a quarterly letter of news, pictures and devotional thoughts to all the alumni whose addresses I had.

The area I covered is approximately the size of the continental United States. But it is 99% ocean and only 1% (or less) land! I traveled by 727 jet to the various centers, and then from there by small plane, diesel boat, speedboat or outrigger canoe to some of the other islands.

Since I had no permanent home, I didn't need much in the way of possessions. When I left Bethania I gave away most of the old things I had been using there. I stored a few books and materials with Ang and Steve, and the rest of my belongings were just simple clothes (mostly mumus) packed in two suitcases. My printed workshop material I mailed ahead to each location.

I had decided that though I would not set meeting or workshop dates, I would need to be prepared for whatever might develop. Having lived in the islands for many years, I knew a person had to be prepared for anything because requests tend to come up at a moment's notice. Micronesians don't like to write letters, so I seldom heard from anyone before going to their islands.

A very important part of the ministry was visitation of the alumni. I tried to see as many of them as possible in each place. This gave me the opportunity to do a lot of counseling. As others besides the alumni came to know me, they also came for counseling. The church leaders began to ask me to speak to various groups on different occasions. In some places, I was busy from the moment of arrival to departure time! As time went on, I was asked to do workshops for other groups besides the alumni. One trip, I did five workshops in Chuuk alone.

What was it like—this itinerant ministry? In a letter home I tried to give a feeling for it by expressing my impressions and meditations:

... watching ten geckoes fight over the flies clustered inside the screen, and being thankful to the Lord for small things like geckoes that help you out in times of need.

... walking up to a group of children on their way to Sunday morning church service, only to find them gambling with their Sunday School offering right at the church steps ... grieving inside over a lifestyle that combines compulsory church attendance with compulsive gambling.

... hearing the story about a man on this same island: "On Christmas Day he came to church bragging to everyone that the night before he had no special Christmas offering, so he had gambled for it. He told everyone that he would lead the 'Christmas dance' into the church and put his offering in first. Before he reached the offering plate that morning, he dropped dead!". . . marveling at the Lord's longsuffering, but longing that these people would understand that God cannot be mocked.

... enjoying the high-pitched, loud and earnest singing of the big choir in white dresses with their crocheted slips hanging below and their offering stuck in their ears ... wondering if they personally know the Lord about whom they are singing and for whom they are so beautifully dressed.

... savoring once again the delicious food of a Micronesian feast given in your honor ... feeling very small and undeserving of all the love demonstrated by these very generous islanders.

... lying awake listening to the heavy breathing of the father and mother and four children in whose room you are sleeping; and watching another rat (or is it the same one that ran across your body a few minutes ago?) come stealthily across the floor in your direction ... be-

ing grateful as you awaken in the morning that the Lord
answered your prayers, keeping the rats from biting those
little children and you.

. . . sitting in the large church, waiting for the women
to come for their meeting and talking inwardly to the
Lord about the church, when suddenly you are startled
by a voice inside you that says, "This is not a church! It's
a cemetery!". . . sorrowing deeply as you view this "Christianity" from God's standpoint, and asking Him once
again to raise the dead.

. . . listening as a woman pours out her hurt, frustration and guilt over her broken relationship with her brothers and sisters in Christ . . . praising God for giving you
His words of wisdom and healing for her, and weeping
together over the victory He gives as she humbly obeys
Him.

. . . waiting once again for a meeting to start (7 o'clock
was the announced time—it's now 9:30!) . . . longing to
always be wise about these waiting times—to use them
to wait upon the Lord in prayer and Bible study or conversation about the things of the Lord with the handful
that may be waiting with you.

. . . reading a letter from one of the alumnae who
writes that three of the couples who attended the Family
Workshop last year have decided, after years of living
together, to be married in church; and that one of the
couples, who were unbelievers, have given their hearts
to the Lord . . . weeping tears of joy before the Lord for
His faithfulness in bringing fruit as He promised from
the teaching of His Word.

. . . sighing as you face once again the job of re-sort-
ing your few things, storing some and packing others in
preparation for the next trip tomorrow . . . singing with
joy in your heart to the Lord for His goodness in letting
you be a small part of His great work.

. . . hearing the nighttime sounds of someone running, being slapped, screaming out in anger (or pain?) a

name that you recognize . . . wondering if you should venture out to see if you can help, knowing it's wiser to stay inside and pray . . . being relieved the next day to find out that though you lost some sleep, nothing serious happened to the girl except that she was drunk and very much needs the Lord's help.

. . . standing before a room full of people who have already sacrificed ten hours this week to learn more about themselves and the Lord . . . feeling totally inadequate to help them, and yet having the assurance that the Holy Spirit can and will meet their needs as you rely totally on Him and walk in obedience to Him.

Twice during my travels in 1982 I made emergency trips back to Guam. Steve and Angela were expecting their second child. Since the baby would have to be delivered by caesarean section, Angela had gone to Guam two months early—while she was still allowed to fly. Steve followed her later.

I was in Saipan when I received the first call. "Angela's in the hospital in labor, five weeks early! They are trying to stop her labor." It was Steve calling for help since he was alone with Ang and Jessica, who was then two years old. I caught a late night flight back to Guam to help out. The Lord was gracious; the labor finally stopped, and both mother and child were O.K. Kurtis was born about six weeks later, on his great-grandmother's 80th birthday, which greatly pleased my mother!

I stayed in Guam to help Angela during her recuperation. What a joy and privilege to be able to be with her instead of 9000 miles away as I was at Jessica's birth. I thoroughly enjoyed my two little grandchildren and loved helping with them. When Kurtis was two weeks old, Angela encouraged me to go on with my travels since everyone was doing fine. They planned to leave for Palau in a few days. I left for Pohnpei.

The second call came my third day in Pohnpei. It was Steve again. "Angela is back in the hospital in serious condition. When the doctor was doing an examination he accidentally punctured her colon without knowing it. I really need your help!"

The Air Micronesia people were able to get me on the first plane to Guam because of the emergency. For the next week, Steve and I took turns in Angela's hospital room with her or in the Mission guest apartment with the two little children. Angela had been nursing Kurtis but had to stop because of her serious condition. It was a difficult time for both of them.

It was hard to see Angela going through so much suffering in such a short period of time. I felt guilty, sitting by her bedside with my strong body while she had to deal with pain and disappointment. We were, however, deeply grateful to the Lord for sparing her life!

I was very proud of my daughter when she was able to readily forgive the negligent doctor. Steve explained to those in charge that while he wouldn't consider suing them for negligence, because we are Christians, that he would expect them to pay the necessary costs, which they did. After a few weeks of recuperation, Steve, Angela and my two grandchildren returned to their work in Palau, and I continued on with my travels.

In 1983 Sandy and Rose were able to come out from Oregon to Palau for a vacation. It was so special—being together once again as a family after three years of separation. Rose had never traveled much before, so it was an eye-opening trip for her. She fell in love with the islands.

The Holy Spirit was faithfully and quietly doing His work as people prayed at home and I obeyed on the field!

17

TORN BETWEEN TWO WORLDS

"For here have we no continuing city, but we seek one to come."—Heb. 13:14 (KJV)

"*I* don't mind if I have to stay overnight here in Minneapolis. I appreciate your offer of a room and dinner. But I am worried about my daughter and son-in-law who are on their way to the airport in Atlanta, or may be already there. They will be several hours from home, and my daughter is expecting any time. They won't be able to return to northern Georgia and then back to Atlanta tomorrow."

Standing in a long line of angry airline passengers, I wanted to speak kindly and not be intimidating. The airline personnel had already been screamed at by several people. I felt sorry for them. It certainly wasn't their personal fault that the plane in Seattle had had "mechanical problems." I was thinking, "It's a good thing these people don't live in Micronesia where we *always* have delays! I guess they would have shouted even louder if they had started this trip as I did in Guam; then through Narita, Japan, with several hours of layover; a 15-hour trip on to Seattle, with the delay there; and finally on to Minneapolis—to miss the plane to Atlanta! Americans are certainly not very patient or understanding."

A voice broke into my thoughts. "Ma'am? We will be glad to have your daughter and son-in-law paged in Atlanta to let them know about the delay." "Thank you so much. I appreciate your help." Actually I found out the next day that the airline personnel had gone the second mile by offering to pay half the cost of Steve and Angela's motel room so they could stay overnight in Atlanta to meet me in the morning.

I wrote to friends later:

> It seems to me that I have left my world to be at the "end of the earth" here in the U.S.! . . . I'm glad that I was able to come when I did because eight days after my arrival I had a new granddaughter! Kristin Melissa was born December 16th, weighing in at 6 pounds 10 ounces and as pretty as a picture! We're all so grateful that everyone is doing fine.
>
> We celebrated our Christmas together here in Hiawassee, Georgia, where Steve's parents have a lovely home. Now Steve and Ang and I are in the midst of planning an itinerary of travel for two and a half months. If the Lord wills, we three adults with the three children will leave Hiawassee on February 14 to travel 6000 miles, arriving in Westbrook, Connecticut, on April 19 for a week's visit with our relatives. It sounds like a rather colossal undertaking, doesn't it?

It was not an easy task: living in people's homes with three little children; trying to keep them happy and entertained during endless miles of travel; juggling them between us in meetings as each of us took part in our presentation of the work in the islands. The Lord was gracious, however. He protected us on the road; gave us wonderful fellowship with our supporting churches and individuals, friends and relatives; and helped us to make new contacts for financial and prayer support.

Attempting to help people understand what a furlough is like for missionaries, I wrote the following letter in the middle of 1985:

> How would you define a missionary's furlough? I've heard Micronesians call it: *"A year-long vacation!"* Missionaries often call it: *"A long year of hard work!"* Since you are my friend, I'd like to share with you some of my feelings about furlough:
>
> Sometimes I get really tired of living out of a suit-

case. . . . Other times I love the opportunity to travel and see different places.

Sometimes I thoroughly enjoy all the rich and delicious food. . . . Other times I hate the constant struggle with my weight.

Sometimes it's a real joy to get to talk with so many people. . . . Other times I wish I could just be alone with my thoughts and my books for a while.

Sometimes I am thrilled at getting all those wonderful letters. . . . Other times I get sick of carrying around all those unanswered letters in my briefcase.

Sometimes I am so happy about getting to see loved friends and relatives again. . . . Other times I am sad that I must once more say good-bye for a few years.

Sometimes I am so thankful for all the opportunities God gives for speaking. . . . Other times I am so pleased that I have a whole week with no meetings.

Sometimes I rejoice in all the sights and sounds that are America, my country. . . . Other times I am very homesick for the tropical ocean, palms, and people that are my adopted country, Micronesia.

•   •   •

January of 1986 found me on my way back to Micronesia. My mother had graciously arranged for the two of us to take a cruise around the Hawaiian Islands for relaxation and fun. We were both looking forward to it. Mother flew there directly from Florida. I was to arrive in Honolulu ahead of her from Oregon, where I had been spending some time with Sandy and Rose. Unfortunately, Portland was having one of those foggy mornings. No planes were taking off! Finally, Sandy decided to drive me to Seattle in hopes that I could get a flight from there. I did. But as the plane was gliding in toward Oahu, I looked down and saw a cruise ship leaving the harbor! Fortunately, the tour people put me into a hotel for two nights until they could transport me by small plane to Hilo, where the ship had moored. In spite of a poor beginning, the cruise was delightful.

On my seven-hour flight from Hawaii to Guam I was lost for a while in contemplation of how my relationship with my mother had changed over the years. Completely fractured for six long years in which I didn't see her at all, it had been mending slowly but surely.

I recalled the letter I had received from Mother when I was a freshman at Providence Bible Institute. It was the first communication from her since she had left. There was still a great knot of bitterness and anger in my heart toward her. I had vowed that I would never again have anything to do with her. Strangely enough, at the same time I was praying for her!

Looking at the return address on the envelope, I recognized Mother's name. Not deigning to even open it, I crumpled it up and threw it in the wastebasket. Before it had hardly hit the basket, I heard an inner voice say, "So you are going to be a missionary! You're going to travel someplace far away and help the people there find Jesus. Who will help your mother find Him?" Stricken with grief, I pulled the letter out of the basket and read it. Mother wanted me to visit her sometime.

That beginning led to an occasional visit in the home of my mother and stepfather. I began the process of forgiveness. Later, after John and I were married, Mother occasionally visited us, or we visited them. More than once I thought I had completely forgiven my mother for the pain and hurt, only to find that it would come up again like a partially healed wound that once more ruptures.

Of course, after we went to the field we saw little of Mother. However, through the years she was able to come out to Palau three times for a week's visit. It was helpful to her to be able to experience my real situation. On my furloughs she would often travel part of the way with me so that she could also visit the relatives I was seeing. She generously helped me a number of times with needs that I had: clothing, a Toyota on my second furlough, a computer with accessories on my fourth furlough, the cruise around the Hawaiian

Islands, etc. I was very grateful for her help.

It was while I was teaching at Bethania that I finally came to grips with the fact that my forgiveness of my mother was not thorough. When I dug deeply into my feelings, I discovered that there was still a pocket of pus that needed to be cleaned out. With the Lord's help, I was able to totally exonerate Mother from all guilt regardless of what she had done. In my heart I declared her innocent, just as the Lord had done for me when I came to Him for forgiveness from my many sins. This freed me to love her in a way I had not done before. The fact remained that my mother and I had quite a different set of values, but I could pray for her with far more empathy than I had had in the past.

After the cruise, when Mother flew back from Honolulu to Florida and I traveled on to Palau for my fifth term, I did not expect to see her again for four years. Mother's eyesight had failed badly and I knew that she would not be able to come out to Palau again. Little did I suspect that I would be traveling to *her* in only eight months!

•   •   •

I was thankful to be back in my home islands of Palau. Once again I threw myself into the ministry to the alumni and the churches there.

In Ngchesar—I stayed with Elizabeth in her house built on mangrove stilts over the water. I watched with joy as the new believers (former young drunkards) searched in their Bibles to find the place for the Bible study. I knew that some would walk village paths in the darkness for an hour to get home.

In Melekeok—I stared with amazement at the elaborate city plan for the future capital of Palau, wishing that the money had been spent on a generator for electricity for this village, or a better dam, so that water hours could be more than one hour a day to fill your drums. As I visited with Risko I rejoiced while observing the new light in her eyes, since she has returned to the Lord. How I praised the Father as thirty-five people gathered in spite of the still, hot night—made hotter by three pressure lamps—and a floor black with mosquitoes, to learn how to submit their will to God's will.

In Ngiwal—I stayed with Francisca, grateful for how her sister's kidney is now working inside *her*, thanks to a prayer-answering God. I visited Lillian, noticing how thin she was, and searching for words of comfort concerning the loss of her second baby. Preaching on Sunday morning in the church, I was saddened to sense a real need of revival here where the work of God first started in Palau fifty-seven years ago.

Then I took off in the speedboat at 6 A.M. to go up the coast to Ngerchelong to attend the Church Leaders' Conference there. Between conference sessions I walked the long, hot road to Rriil to see alumnae; got caught in a brief but heavy shower; and walked barefoot through the red mud to get back. I was deeply moved—to tears—as I shared my feelings about the faithfulness of our great God before the congregation and conference, seeing among them Sakeziro and other new believers who had come from Ngerdmau; Gideon and Anemary, whom God had revived, having come from Saipan; and all the faithful men and women of God whom He had raised up through the years.

On the other side of Babeldaob, in Ngermlenguii, I visited Yosie in her house with her children and grandchildren around her, thinking how hard it must be to live in the same village as your ex-husband, who left you for another. After giving my Bible study on Daniel, I heard Yosie pray, "Thank You, Lord, for sending Your servant to help me." As I sat on the floor in the community house on Sunday morning, I marveled at the number of young men and women who had come, and praised God for using His servants to bring revival to this village.

The Father was at work through the islands of Micronesia, and the opportunities for service seemed endless. My primary concern was how to fit into my time all the ministries that waited to be done.

18

INTO THE CLOSET

"Come, My people, enter your chambers and shut your doors behind you; hide yourselves for a little while."—Isa. 26:20a (Amp.)

"*L*EAVE MICRONESIA? But I can't! I won't! Please don't make me leave Micronesia!"

I was spending a few weeks in Guam, putting out letters to the alumni and folks back home, and preparing for my trip through eastern Micronesia. I had finished my ministries for 1986 in Palau, Yap, Saipan and Guam. It was nearing time to leave for Chuuk, Pohnpei, Kosrae, Ebeye and Majuro.

For months I had been reading and praying about the deeper life. I had a longing to totally abandon "self" and give up my will once and for all in complete submission to the Father's will. I knew that intercession was the key to revival in Micronesia, but felt that I was lacking in that area though I kept trying to be a devoted intercessor.

I was studying Norman Grubb's book entitled: *Rees Howells, Intercessor.*[1] I had come to admire and wanted to emulate that great Welsh prayer warrior. In the story of the life of Rees Howells I found that the prerequisite to being greatly used by God was death to self. That was not a new concept for me. I had "died to self" a number of times, but only found my self soon "rising from the dead" again. Now I had finally come to grapple with real "death."

I found as I studied Romans 8:5–14 that I could not live *"in accordance with the Spirit"* as long as part of me was think-

---

[1] Norman Grubb, *Rees Howells, Intercessor;* Fort Washington, PA, Christian Literature Crusade, 1952.

ing according to the flesh. The flesh had to die! As I tried to understand what it literally means to die to self, the Lord brought certain scriptures to my attention.

"The land on which your feet have walked will be your inheritance and that of your children forever, because you have followed the Lord my God wholeheartedly."—Josh. 14:9. It was Caleb quoting the words of Moses. I thought of Caleb, that champion of faith, who had followed the Lord wholeheartedly at age forty and was still following at eighty-five when he spoke these words. What did it mean to follow the Lord wholeheartedly? For Caleb as a young man it meant being in the hated minority for the sake of the Lord's plans. As an old man it meant having the courage to fight against the fortified cities in the hill country and to destroy the giants. Caleb was ready to go through war with its bloodshed, pain, heartache, suffering, discomfort. No half-hearted effort would do here! This must be part of dying to self.

The Lord also showed me that dying to self meant willingness to be a true disciple. It was being putty in the hands of the Lord so that He could teach and use me. But there was a cost: *"If anyone comes to Me and does not hate his father and mother, his wife and children, his brothers and sisters—yes, even his own life—he cannot be My disciple. And anyone who does not carry his cross cannot be My disciple. . . . In the same way, any of you who does not give up everything he has cannot be My disciple."*—Luke 14:26–27, 33. Of course, I knew these verses well. But had I really given up my life, taken up my cross, however painful, and turned over everything I had and was to the Father?

The Lord summarized my struggle with the reality of self by asking, "Can you drink My cup? Remember, *'whoever wants to be first must be a slave!'"*—Matt. 20:22, 25–28. I realized that I was battling the necessity of giving up all rights. I loved the Lord and desired to please Him, but somehow I also wanted to keep some of my rights.

He reminded me that death is the only way to produce fruit. *"I tell you the truth, unless a kernel of wheat falls to the ground and dies, it remains only a single seed. But if it dies it produces many seeds."*—John 12:24. Following Jesus meant going to the cross, dying, falling into the ground.

"To this you were called, because Christ suffered for you, leaving you an example, that you should follow in His steps. . . . When they hurled their insults at Him, He did not retaliate; when He suffered, He made no threats. Instead, He entrusted Himself to Him who judges justly."—1 Peter 2:21, 23. So it was to this that I was being called! I took a long hard look at the reality of dying and decided that I could not turn away from the Lord's call, but must deliver all that I was into His hands to be put to death.

It was a greater struggle than I had imagined. But finally it was over, and I could say to my Father, *"O Lord, my God, other lords besides You have ruled over me* (including self) . . . *they are now dead, they live no more"* (taken from Isa. 26:13 and 14).

The Lord wasted no time in testing this complete commitment to losing all my rights to Him![2]

The following day I received a letter from my sister-in-law in which she told me that Mother had suffered an eyestroke. Although it had seemingly not harmed her body, it had destroyed the eyesight in her only good eye. My brother had moved her from Florida to Texas to be near them, since she had now been declared legally blind.

Reading the letter, my heart went out to my mother in her trouble. I was also concerned about my brother and his wife, since they were caring for her mother as well. "What shall I do, Lord?" I asked.

I felt the answer I dreaded: "Leave Micronesia. Go and take care of your mother."

How could I leave Micronesia? My home for twenty-four years, this was the most precious place on earth to me. I knew I could take care of Mother, and I didn't mind doing that. *But how could I leave Micronesia?*

For several days I wept and prayed most of the time. It

---

[2] See principle #25, Appendix.

was the Lord who had called me to these islands. I thought the call was for life. Could this really be His will—that I leave the great opportunities that were opening up before me? I talked to no one about my dilemma. I wanted only to hear from the Lord, for fear someone else might confuse the issue. This decision was too important to take chances on being misled.

As always, the Lord was faithful to show me beyond the shadow of a doubt what His thinking was. He reminded me of what I had been teaching in my workshops the past few months. The subject of the Bible study segment was the life of Joseph. I had taught with great emphasis the importance of forgiveness as lived out in Joseph's life. I had pointed out that the final step that Joseph had to take in the path of forgiveness of his brothers was to personally care for them.

After Jacob's death, Joseph's ten brothers were afraid. Suppose that he still held a secret grudge against them and would now get his revenge—with his father no longer there to see it? When they came in fear to Joseph, asking for mercy, he wept and said, *"'Don't be afraid. Am I in the place of God? You intended to harm me, but God intended it for good to accomplish what is now being done, the saving of many lives. So then, don't be afraid. I will provide for you and your children.' Then he reassured them and spoke kindly to them."*—Gen. 50:19–21.

The Lord told me that what I had been teaching others I now had the opportunity to apply to my life. I was to take the final step in forgiveness of my mother by going to take care of her.

The Father used other scriptures to speak to me as well:

*"Is it not to share your food with the hungry and to provide the poor wanderer with shelter—when you see the naked, to clothe him, and **not to turn away from your own flesh and blood?**"*—Isa. 58:7.

"Yet it was the Lord's will to crush Him and cause Him to suffer . . . and the will of the Lord will prosper in his hand. . . . He made intercession for the transgressors."—Isa. 53:10–12.

"Today if you hear His voice, do not harden your hearts as you

did at Meribah, as you did that day at Massah in the desert, where your fathers tested and tried Me, though they had seen what I did." —Psa. 95:8–9.

I had seen what the Lord had done. He had done great things in Micronesia and wonderful things in my family. Only a few days earlier He had done a special work in my life, bringing me to a deeper relationship with Him. If I hardened my heart now, I would be going back on the covenant I had made to give up my rights to Him. And with a hardened heart, I would not be able to fulfill His purposes for me.

I finally whispered, "Yes, Lord. I believe You are asking me to leave Micronesia to take care of my mother. I don't understand why, and I don't know if You will ever let me return, but I submit my will to Yours. I will do as You ask." I felt like those whom Isaiah had written about: *"Lord, they came to You in their distress; when You disciplined them, they could barely whisper a prayer."*—Isa. 26:16.[3]

As I continued reading in Isaiah 26, I was reminded of how the intercession God had been speaking to me about was like giving birth—painful but productive: *"As a woman with child and about to give birth writhes and cries out in her pain, so were we in Your presence, O Lord."*—Isa. 26:17. That intercession would bring life! *"But your dead will live; their bodies will rise. You who dwell in the dust, wake up and shout for joy."*—Isa. 26:19.

How is this travail accomplished? Jesus had said, *"When you pray, go into your room, close the door and pray to your Father, who is unseen. Then your Father who sees what is done in secret will reward you."*—Matt. 6:6. So the Father was saying to me, "Go into your closet and pray"—which tied in with Isaiah 26:20. He showed me that He was taking me out of public ministry *to* Micronesians to put me into a closet where I could seriously intercede *for* Micronesians!

I answered the Lord with some verses from one of my favorite psalms: *"Lord, You have assigned me my portion and my cup. . . . I have set the Lord always before me. Because He is at my*

---

[3] See principle #26, Appendix.

right hand, I will not be shaken."—Psa. 16:5a, 8.

Then the Father encouraged me with the assurance that obedience to Him would result in victory in Micronesia: *"The Sovereign Lord will wipe away the tears from all faces; He will remove the disgrace of His people from all the earth. The Lord has spoken. They will say, 'Surely this is our God; we trusted in Him and He saved us. This is the Lord, we trusted in Him; let us rejoice and be glad in His salvation.'. . . He will bring down your high fortified walls and lay them low; He will bring them down to the ground, to the very dust."*—Isa. 25:8–9, 12.

I was greatly encouraged to be reminded that intercession could "bring down the walls." The Lord had spoken to us about those walls before we ever went to the islands, and I had seen and felt the evidence of them in my ministry.

So the decision was made. When my mother, brother and sister-in-law heard that I had decided to return to care for Mother, they were quite surprised. No one had asked me to do it. The news was a blow to Angela. She wept as I had, because I was leaving Micronesia and my missionary work.

In a letter to everyone back home and on the field, I tried to explain by using three pictures:

God is weaving the pattern of my life! In these pictures you see Benina in the process of weaving *a very ordinary but extremely useful basket* out of coconut fronds; Ritsko and Rosamistica learning to weave *lovely and strong purses* from pandanus; and the alumni from Ngchesar meeting for Bible study under *a simple but protective roof* woven of coconut fronds.

God is at work in our lives weaving something. It may be ordinary but useful, lovely and strong, or simple but protective. *"In a large house there are articles not only of gold and silver, but also of wood and clay."*—2 Tim. 2:20.

So what shall we do when we don't like the thing God is asking us to do? He is making us into a simple basket or a clay pot, and we want to be a lovely purse or a cup of gold. Do we have a right to question His design? *"Woe to the man who fights with his Creator. Does the pot argue with his maker? Does the clay dispute with him who forms it, saying, 'Stop, you're doing it wrong!' or the pot exclaim, 'How clumsy can you be!'?"*—Isa. 45:9 (TLB).

The Lord reminds us in Isaiah 46:9–11: "*I am God, and there is no other. . . . My purpose will stand, and I will do all that I please . . . what I have planned, that I will do.*"

How far do you think Benina, Ritsko and Rosamistica would get in their weaving if the pandanus and coconut fronds were alive and resisting? It would take a lot longer to make the useful or beautiful object they planned. A quiet, submissive frond is a joy to the Creator, making it possible for Him to quickly fulfill His wise plans in *"bringing many sons to glory."*—Heb. 2:10.

So I have submitted my self and my will to the Father because I desire to please Him by being *"an instrument for noble purposes, made holy, useful to the Master and prepared to do any good work."*—2 Tim. 2: 21b.

In the plane on my way back to the U.S., I was blessed in the study of Psalm 116. Certain verses especially touched my heart: *"The cords of death* (to self) *entangled me, the anguish of the grave came upon me. . . . Then I called on the name of the Lord: 'O Lord, save me!' . . . Be at rest once more, O my soul, for the Lord has been good to you. . . . Precious in the sight of the Lord is the 'death' of His saints. O Lord, truly I am Your servant. . . . You have freed me from my chains. . . . I will fulfill my vows to the Lord in the presence of all His people."*

I decided to stop in Oregon on my way east to see Sandy and Rose. They were expecting their first child any day, and I hoped to make it in time for the birth. As it turned out I missed the deadline, but the home birth of Carissa Ann went smoothly, and I got there in time to see her when only a few days old. She was so cute and bright that I thought she must be a month old already! How rich I was to have four grandchildren to love!

While I was in their home the Lord gave me some promises in my devotional times:

*"'For I know the thoughts and plans that I have for you,'
says the Lord, 'thoughts and plans for welfare and peace, and
not for evil, to give you hope in your final outcome. Then you
will call upon Me, and you will come and pray to Me, and I
will hear and heed you. Then you will seek Me, inquire for and
require Me (as a vital necessity) and find Me; when you search
for Me with all your heart, I will be found by you,' says the
Lord, 'and I will release you from captivity and gather you
from all the nations and all the places to which I have driven
you,' says the Lord, 'and I will bring you again to the place
from which I caused you to be carried away captive.'"*—Jer.
29:11–14 (Amp.).

*"I am God, the God of your father; do not be afraid to go
down to Egypt* (the United States?); *for I will there make of
you a great nation* (through intercession?). *I will go down
with you to Egypt, and **I will surely bring you up again.**"*—
Gen. 46:3–4a (Amp.).

What a great comfort it was to me to know that someday,
though I had no idea when, the Lord would take me back to
my "home" from which I was now exiled. This made it much
easier for me to go on in obedience to do what the Lord had
asked.

I flew from Oregon to New Jersey to explain face-to-face
at the Mission headquarters why I had left the field. I assured
the Director that I hoped to return to Micronesia someday,
and that I would like to continue on as a Liebenzell missionary on extended furlough. I smiled when he mentioned that
he would like me to consider being the Overseas Director in
the future. I had no intention of taking on such a title and
responsibility. I explained that my first priority was to care
for my mother, so I did not feel free to take on anything else.
I was not aware that, in time, this picture would change dras-
tically!

19

UNFAMILIAR PATHS

"I will lead the blind by ways they have not known, along unfamiliar paths I will guide them; I will turn the darkness into light before them and make the rough places smooth. These are the things I will do; I will not forsake them."—Isa. 42:16

*I*n November 1986, I wrote from Amarillo, Texas, to friends: "Thank you for praying for my mother. She is taking her disability well. She has enough light in one eye to be able to do a number of things for herself. Of course, she needs help in many things. *Please pray that she will draw closer to God, and that I will patiently and lovingly care for her."*

My brother and I had been praying for my mother for forty-five years. Although for some time she had attended church when she was with us, and we often talked about the Lord in her presence, we felt that she had never committed herself to Christ. It was a heavy burden to us, especially as we watched her health deteriorate and her years increase. It was my desire that as I lived with her I would be able to saturate our small apartment with prayer, thus inviting the Holy Spirit's presence.

I felt that the Lord had given me a promise for my mother in Isaiah 42:16. I was trusting that in time He would *"turn her darkness into light"* and make her *"rough places smooth."* I knew that she was now traveling down *"unfamiliar paths,"* living with a committed Christian missionary. I wanted to be sensitive to her in this radical lifestyle change. In retrospect, I wish I could say that I had achieved that goal, but I'm afraid that I often failed.

WALKING THE WAVES

Part of my failure was due to the fact that I, too, was now traveling "unfamiliar paths." For twenty-four years I had been in ministry, usually in leadership of some kind. Now I found myself sitting in the congregation of a huge church, unknown and knowing no one except my three family members there. Added to my loneliness for my children and grandchildren, and my intense homesickness for Micronesia, was my unful-filled longing to be in ministry. I finally was able in prayer to reconcile myself to sitting and listening, lost in the crowd and feeling very alien. I was comforted by the Lord's promise: *"You will know which way to go, since you have never been this way before. . . . Consecrate yourselves, for tomorrow the Lord will do amazing things among you."*—Josh. 3:4–5. What an encour-agement to be assured that the Lord had plans to do *"amazing things"* at some *"tomorrow."*

In time the Lord allowed me to do some limited ministry in Amarillo. I explained it in one of my letters:

I joined the choir. Pray that my voice and visage will bring light! I had the thrill of being "one of the ornaments" on the Living Christmas Tree at the First Baptist Church. It was a lot of work, but such fun, climbing the 40-foot tree for eight performances. And what an opportunity to minister to some ten to twelve thousand people, through music and words, the magic of "the Word made flesh." Each evening I worshiped the Lord on that tree, espe-cially while listening to the singing of the beautiful duet about the "ten thousand joys" which are brought to my life by my wonderful Lord.

In March of 1987 I wrote to friends about Mother's first heart attack:

I believe that your prayers are the reason that she is still with us. On February 22nd she was in much pain and had trouble breathing. We rushed her to the hospi-tal. Her blood pressure had gone off the scale! Because the nurses and doctors acted fast, and her body responded well to the medication, she was saved from death. At her age and condition, however, she could easily have another attack. Please continue to pray for her, and especially that *she will be ready to meet the Lord when the time comes.*

The Father had opened up a small door of ministry to me which gave me much joy. I began teaching a Sunday School class of Laotian and Vietnamese teenagers. Twice a week I taught English to a variety of internationals. That was a challenge—especially with those who were new in the country! Sometimes I gave the devotional message for all the internationals who attended the English classes. Among them were Buddhists, Hindus and Spiritists. What a privilege it was to be able to present Jesus Christ to them!

In my letter of May 1987 I wrote:

Mother has had another heart attack. She spent nine days in the hospital. She has had more heart damage and is much weaker than before. She can walk only short distances, so we use the wheelchair a lot. Thank you for your prayers for her, and for me as I care for her.

People who think missionaries only suffer and sacrifice definitely don't see the whole picture! As always, along with multiple problems, my family and I were being showered with blessings from a generous and gracious God.

About Angela and Steve I wrote:

They were blessed with the opportunity of making a round-the-world trip this summer. They were able to accomplish the purposes of this mini-furlough: medical attention for Angela; deputation in some of their supporting churches; and visitation of many of their relatives.

About Sandy and Rose I wrote:

They were able to fly over to Amarillo from Oregon to spend time with and care for Mother. Thanks to Mother's generosity, they flew on to New Jersey to be with the rest of us there for two weeks. We had long family conferences, attempting to pool our brain power to think of ways in which Sandy and Rose can carry out the call they feel to serve the Lord in the islands.

My life was also beginning to curve around toward a different direction. The Lord began to urge me to help in needs that the Mission was experiencing. While I was at the Board of Directors retreat in New Jersey, I was asked to take the position of Overseas Personnel Coordinator. It involved working with missionaries on the field, as well as inquirers, candidates and appointees in the U.S., using the phone, fax, computer and letters, as I continued caring for Mother.

As part of my new responsibility as Overseas Personnel Coordinator, I was sent by the Board to attend the meetings of the Council of Liebenzell Mission International which took place in Japan. I wrote to friends:

It was an interesting trip. There was very little time for sightseeing, but I did get to eat some fabulous Japanese food, including my favorite—sashimi (raw fish). I met some wonderful Japanese pastors and got to give my testimony in one of their churches. But all of that was minor compared to what the Lord taught me while I was there attending meetings with our National Directors from the U.S., Germany, Canada and Switzerland, and Area Directors from our fields in Micronesia, Papua New Guinea, Manus, Bangladesh, Japan, Taiwan and Zambia.

Although I didn't realize it at the time, I can see now that the Lord was preparing me with these experiences for His next assignment.

In May 1988 I wrote to friends and supporters about another preparatory experience the Lord was giving me:

I am in the process of planning our Candidate Orientation, to take place June 25 through July 10. It will be a time when we try to prepare our candidates and appointees for the work ahead. We will have an anthropologist, a psychologist, Mission leaders, pastors and missionaries there in New Jersey for two weeks to try to pass on some of their expertise in serving the Lord in cross-cultural situations. We trust that our new people will gain many insights into the Lord and about themselves and the people whom they will be serving.

By August of that year I had turned all the way around to the new direction toward which the Lord had been leading me. My children and their families were going through or heading toward major changes as well.

Steve and Angela had moved to Guam, where Steve was the interim Area Director for Liebenzell Mission in Micronesia. They were expecting an addition in March. And Sandy and Rose had applied to become Liebenzell missionaries!

I also had two big news items: When I was at the Mission headquarters in July, I was appointed as Director of Overseas Ministries. That job included all that I had been doing as Overseas Personnel Coordinator, plus more responsibility for the welfare of our missionaries and fields, as well as development into new fields.

I explained in a letter how I felt when I sensed God's call to accept this great honor and burden:

> When I was studying the early life of Saul recently, I could really empathize with him when *"he hid himself among the baggage."*—1 Sam. 10:22. There are times when I would like to hide myself in Micronesia! But then there is the Lord's call to fill this gap at this time. I was encouraged as I thought of how the Spirit of the Lord came upon Saul, giving him a new heart, and I, too, found my calling: *"Do whatever you find to be done, for God is with you."*—1 Sam. 10:6–9.
>
> The problem is that I can't do it alone! But reading on, I discovered that *"there went with him a band of valiant men whose hearts God had touched."*—1 Sam. 10:26. Will you help me pray that there will be some "valiant person" who will be willing to help with this big responsibility?

My second news item: Mother's health was much improved, so she had decided to return to Florida. When she did, there was no longer a reason for me to stay in Amarillo, so I moved to New Jersey to be near the headquarters.[1]

Meanwhile, Mother continued to give generously to all her family members, making it possible for my all-mission-ary side of the family to be provided for in a way we had never expected. When I was younger, I vowed that I would never accept anything from my mother because of the way she had failed and hurt me. During my time living with Mother, the Lord showed me that part of my forgiveness of her meant that I needed to graciously accept her offers of help and express my sincere appreciation for her kindness to my children and me.

Mother provided financially not only for her children and grandchildren, but also set up a trust fund for the college edu-cation of her great-grandchildren. My faithful brother became her trustee and took care of all Mother's finances. The Lord blessed us through Mother's generosity and Sax's hard work and willingness to serve the rest of the family. My disappoint-ment and sadness over my mother has been changed to deep gratitude and appreciation to her for all her help.

The greatest thankfulness I feel, however, is to the Lord for answering my prayers of fifty-four years for Mother's sal-vation. In order to complete this saga of my relationship with my mother, I will jump ahead to May 1994. By that time Mother was living in a retirement residence in Amarillo, where she was diagnosed with inoperable cancer. I flew back from Guam to spend a month with her. It was a good time of fel-lowship in spite of Mother's health restrictions. I was very burdened with the desire to talk to her again about seeking God's forgiveness and committing herself to Him. I had tried many times through the years, but she had always seemed to resent my bringing up the subject. I wanted to speak to her in an inoffensive and loving way, so I asked the Lord to give me a special opportunity to do that.

One night while we were watching TV a Billy Graham Special came on. Mother wasn't really interested, but when I

---

[1] See principle #27, Appendix.

requested that we watch it, she finally acquiesced. By the time the program was coming to a close with the invitation, I noticed that Mother was wiping away the tears and breathing hard. I prepared her for bed and made her comfortable. Then I began to talk to her about the Lord. I told her that I loved her very much and couldn't bear to think of being in heaven without her. She told me that she had asked Jesus to forgive her and felt sure that she would be there. I committed her to the Lord, trusting that she had made that all-important decision.

I visited Mother once more five months later. She passed away peacefully soon afterward, at the age of 92. When I was young, I never dreamed that I would love and miss my mother so much. The Lord has shown me that He is vitally interested in our family relationships and wants us to do whatever we can to maintain or restore them. When we are willing to humble ourselves, to forgive and seek forgiveness, He will bless us beyond our wildest dreams.

20

An Overwhelming Challenge

"Do not be afraid. Stand firm and you will see the deliverance the Lord will bring you. . . . The Lord will fight for you; you need only to be still."—Exod. 13:13–14

When I moved to New Jersey in November 1988, I began to see that my fears about accepting the job of Director of Overseas Ministries of Liebenzell U.S.A. were well founded. When our International Director called me from Germany to ask how I felt about the new assignment, I told him that I was not interested in title or position, and felt that I was greatly under-qualified. I would have refused the call to serve as Overseas Director if it had not also come from the Lord.

When I had told the Lord that I didn't feel qualified, He simply agreed. He always has this way of being really honest with me when I humbly express my doubts. I had no desire to try to do something at which I was fairly certain to fail. And I have been in enough positions in my life to recognize that the person on top is always blamed first. Besides all that, there was my ever-present longing to be back in Micronesia.

But the need was very obvious to me by this time. Missionaries were discouraged—some near quitting. Appointees were dropping out because of lack of help. There were no new candidates coming up, and not enough people being contacted. There were financial difficulties on all sides—some very serious. The whole situation was crying for someone to help! The Lord showed me that though I couldn't do everything, *I could do something*! If nothing else, I could encourage the fainthearted and help them to stand firm on the field or continue working toward going to the field.

I was excited about being a part of a team which had the potential of actually getting people out to fulfill God's great desire to reach a lost world. I enjoyed the opportunity to interact with all kinds of people on my many travels. But in a letter which I wrote about those travels, I also described my very real discouragement.

I'll be perfectly honest! Some days I feel quite discouraged! It happens when I hear that the missionaries are going through difficult trials. I feel the most discouragement when people whom we have worked with for a long time decide after all that they don't want to serve as missionaries overseas, or when those who are waiting to go cannot find enough prayer and financial supporters. Often my discouragement comes from the realization that this job is way too big for me!

On days like that I can somehow relate to the prophet Jeremiah. The "mire" I sink into is more mental and emotional than the muck he was dropped down into in that abandoned cistern. As we read the story in Jeremiah 38, it is a breath of fresh air to come upon the part where the Ethiopian eunuch named Ebed-Melech intercedes for Jeremiah with the king. Help was on the way with that intercession! When you intercede for me with the King of kings, help will be on the way to get me out of my "mire" of difficulties and discouragement!

But Ebed-Melech did more than speak up for the prophet. He put "feet to his words" by getting some men to help him. They gathered old rags and let them down by ropes into the cistern for Jeremiah to put under his arms so that the ropes by which they would pull him out would be padded. I have such a vivid picture in my mind of that dear black man with his tender, loving touch and care for God's chosen prophet! Tears come to my eyes when I remember people like him who minister to me in my "down times." That loving touch comes to me through your concerned letters and faithful financial support.

I like the way the story ends! In Jeremiah 39:15–18 we hear the Lord Almighty speaking specifically to that Ethiopian eunuch. When all about him are dying, the Lord says to him, "*I will rescue you . . . you will not fall by the sword . . . because you trust in Me.*" Your help in His work does not go unnoticed—by Him or by me!

Some who responded to that letter expressed surprise and/or shock that I experienced and admitted discouragement. I wonder what they would have thought if they knew that for weeks I wept and prayed every night over problems that loomed much larger than the ones mentioned in my letter. Sometimes I felt that I was fighting a losing battle. I discussed it with no one but the Lord. One of those dark nights He assured me that I only needed to "*be still,*" for He would "*fight for me.*"—Exod. 14:13–14.

Another night as I cried out for the future of the Mission, the Lord spoke and I prayed through Jeremiah 31:3–17 in the Amplified Bible. I heard my Father's comforting words about the past and His assurance for the future of the Mission: "*I have loved you with an everlasting love . . . and have continued My faithfulness to you. . . . I will build you, and you shall be built. . . . You shall plant vineyards* (fruit-bearing churches?). *. . . The planters shall plant and shall make the fruit common and enjoy it. . . . Sing aloud with gladness. . . . The Lord has saved His people!*"

The rest of the chapter (verses 9–14) became my prayer. "Lord, bring us together in penitence and prayer. Cause us to walk in a straight way by Your streams of living water. Let the islands and nations rejoice because of Your work in us. Lord, ransom us from our strong enemy. Help us to flow together and rejoice over Your goodness. Make our lives fruitful. Turn our sorrow into joy. Father, amaze us with the offerings You send."

And then on a more personal level, I prayed through verses 16 and 17: "Thank you, Lord, for comforting me as I have been weeping here before You, and for promising to reward my work in this place. Please keep my children from the enemy, and bring them to their 'own country,' Micronesia, in Your time."

The Lord was working toward that goal of bringing my children and grandchildren to serve Him in Guam and Micronesia as He had promised. Ashley, my fifth grandchild, was born to Steve and Angela in February that year as Steve continued to serve as Area Director for Liebenzell Mission in Micronesia. Sandy and Rose were working, praying, and trusting the Lord to supply their financial needs so that they could be out in Guam by the end of August to serve as guest house managers for the Mission.

On July 1st Cassandra (Cassie) Simpson was born in Oregon—at home, with the assistance of Sandy and a midwife—swelling the number of my grandchildren to six!

Sandy's family was able to begin their ministry in Guam as planned by the end of August. The Lord was fulfilling my heart's desires for my children, yet keeping me separated from them by 9000 miles! What strange ways God has at times. For years I was in Micronesia and they were in the U.S.A. Now I was in the U.S.A. and they were in Micronesia!

The Lord was also at work on the home front. As always He kept His promise: *"There went with him a band of valiant men whose hearts God had touched."*—1 Sam. 10:26. One by one, He sent the personnel we needed to be able to get things in order at the headquarters and to move ahead with His worldwide agenda. In answer to my cries for help in the Overseas Department, He sent the first *"valiant"* person, Barbara Cassidy, as secretary/bookkeeper for our department. She became my right arm. What an encouragement she was to me in the years that followed, as we together wept and prayed over the needs of the candidates and missionaries and searched for ways to minister to them. Next, the Lord found Dan Smith, whom we recruited as Business Manager. Then He called Rev. Henry Schriever to serve as Director. Little by little, things improved and problems were solved.

I became increasingly busy as I traveled extensively to

recruit people, attended various board and committee meetings, and wrote hundreds of letters. But one of my primary concerns was for more prayer and fasting at the headquarters. We formed a Prayer Committee which developed plans and programs for the purpose of encouraging more joint prayer among our staff.

We were contacting more and more people to serve as missionaries, but many were having difficulty raising support to get to the field. A few at a time, new people were coming on board. I had never realized before how difficult it is to recruit and find support for new missionaries.

I did a lot of overseas traveling during my service as Overseas Director. In 1990 I was commissioned by the Board of Liebenzell U.S.A. to do some preliminary investigation in Burundi, with the potentiality of opening a new field there for Liebenzell International. I decided to visit our work in France and Zambia on the same trip. I described that trip in my prayer letter, entitled "Musings and Prayers of a Sojourner." Following are excerpts:

At JFK Airport, New York: Is this really me, a little old lady, getting ready to embark on a three-week trip to France and Africa? Lord, I'm scared and honored at the same time. Why me? You know I'm a nobody, and yet You have entrusted me with this responsibility. Please go before me . . . beside me . . . surround me . . . and pour Your life through me.

In Paris, France: The Kopps have been so kind, taking me on a quick tour of the city to see Notre Dame, the Champs Élysées, Eiffel Tower, the Arc de Triomphe. What a historic city! How appropriate that a German came here to France and planted a church on "Avenue May 8, 1945" in Palaiseau. That was the day of the liberation of the French from the Germans! Thank You, Lord, for turning people and nations around.

In Normandy, France: These three young couples (from Liebenzell) certainly have their work cut out for them. It's not easy being a missionary in France, especially a German one! The work is hard and slow, dealing one-on-one with people not very willing to listen.

In Nairobi, Kenya: Wow! That Kenyan took my itinerary of tickets to go find and tag my suitcase for the flight to Bujumbura and to get a boarding pass. I hope he's honest! This could be quite a predicament to find myself with no suitcase or tickets on the eastern side of Africa! Oh, there he is with the boarding pass in his hand. Thank You, Lord! You always take such good care of me.

In Bujumbura, Burundi: There's Mbanda! Praise the Lord! He's the one who first told me about the Rwandese refugees. He knows! He is one.... That was a long road yesterday across Burundi, and my body aches from the jolting ride over dirt roads. Besides that, I've got diarrhea today from the food. *But I am so-o-o thankful!* You answered my prayers to be able to see one of the far-off refugee areas. ... It was a joy to be able to fellowship with some of Mbanda's relatives there in their round mud "hut." Imagine being refugees for 30 years! ... By the way, Lord, thanks so much for keeping me from diarrhea yesterday as I traveled for ten hours with three Rwandese men, and no rest rooms! You are so faithful! ... Yes, Lord, I hear what You are saying about *"a great door for effective work being opened."*—1 Cor. 16:9. If it is indeed Your will that the Liebenzell Mission open a new field here in Burundi, please confirm that through the other leaders.

In Nairobi, Kenya: Again You came to my rescue, Lord. Landing alone here at night, not really knowing where to go, was scary, but You directed me to a Kenetco taxi driver like I was told to look for; he actually knew where to find CPK. They had an extra room and could put me up at that Anglican Guest House; and they fed me supper and breakfast. Thank you!

In Kasama, Zambia: That eight-hour drive up here was wearying, but I sure learned a lot on the way from the German missionaries and Beven (Zambian). They all seemed very worried about the group of armed men who stopped us. I guess it's common here for people to be robbed, raped or killed by these bands of guerillas, especially in out-of-the-way areas. Thank You, Lord, for somehow convincing them not to try anything with us!

In Lusaka, Zambia, heading for New York: Lord, if You carry me through this final day of 40 hours of driving, sitting in airports and flying, I will give You all the glory for all You have done and taught me on this trip!

Arriving home from Africa, I was unable to forget the needs I had witnessed, especially in Burundi. While there, the Lord had touched my heart with these verses:

"I found that the Lord had opened a door for me."—2 Cor. 2:12b.

"This is how we know what love is: Jesus Christ laid down His life for us. And we ought to lay down our lives for our brothers. If anyone has material possessions and sees his brother in need but has no pity on him, how can the love of God be in him?"—1 John 3:16–17.

I found myself wishing that I could split into many persons. One could stay in Burundi, another in Zambia, another in Papua New Guinea, and of course several in the Micronesian Islands! How thankful I am that Liebenzell International now has an active ministry in Burundi.[1]

In 1992, after having served four years as Director of Overseas Ministries, I became aware that the Lord was indicating an upcoming change of direction. I began to spend much time in prayer, soul-searching, and listening to God. One day I was surprised to receive a rather pointed message from Him that made it clear that I was to move on.

---

[1] See principle #28, Appendix.

21

Back Over the Waves

"You have stayed long enough at this mountain."—Deut. 1:6b

*T*his was the Lord's explicit directive to me as I pondered and prayed about my future ministry. When I understood that the Lord wanted me to return to the islands, I requested the Liebenzell Board of Directors to find a replacement for me within a year. My prayer was from Numbers 27:16–17: *"May the Lord, the God of the spirits of all mankind, appoint a man over this community to go out and come in before them, one who will lead them out and bring them in, so the Lord's people will not be like sheep without a shepherd."*[1] I also requested permission to continue on as a full-time missionary past my 65th birthday, and to return to my ministries in Guam and Micronesia.

Finally, in April 1993, I was back in the islands, writing to friends:

> How thankful I am to be holding Josiah, my seventh grandchild, in my arms! I had asked the Lord to have an apartment picked out for me, and I know that many of you were praying that request with me. The day after I arrived Sandy and I went to meet a landlady to look at her soon-to-be-vacated apartment. That was the only one I looked at, because it is perfect! The apartment was vacated April 28th and that's the very day the ship arrived with my things, so my fears about having to store them someplace were taken care of. The Lord always does such a good job!

---

[1] See Principle #29, Appendix.

WALKING THE WAVES

What a special joy it was to be close to both my children and their families! The last time we lived close to each other was 28 years before when the family was together in Palau. It was so good to be back home in "my" islands! My heart was overflowing with gratitude to my Father who always does *"immeasurably more than all we ask or imagine."*—Eph. 3:20.

•   •   •

It's hard to picture the wonder and diversity of Micronesia until you have lived there for a while. Sandy's song, *"Back Over the Waves,"*[2] musically expresses the beauty of the region, as well as the burden God has given my family and me to reach the island peoples.

From the green Palau rock islands, all sparkling in the blue . . .
   To the Pohnpeian waterfalls within the jungle dew . . .
From the many Chuukese villages around the blue lagoon . . .
   To the far-flung outer islands that from God's great hand
               were strewn . . .

From the island of Ulithi to Kosraean paradise . . .
   From the Marianas Trench to Mount Lamlam set on high . . .
From the ancient Yapese culture with its money
               made from stone . . .
   To the atolls of the Marshalls . . . the Truth must now be shown!

From the Banzai Cliffs of Saipan to Red Beach of Peleliu . . .
   From the strings of emerald islands to Helen's Reef, Ngulu . . .
From Guam's bustling tourist hotels to deserted island beach . . .
   From the hundreds and the thousands of island people
               in our reach . . .

From the ocean swells that wander and shatter on the shores . . .
   To the seagulls flying over, seeking refuge from the storms . . .
From the workers in the gardens to the fishermen at sea . . .
   From the old men walking slowly to the children running free . . .

We are the Body of Jesus, the Church of Christ the Lord.
   We're building faith on one Foundation, and trusting in His Word.
We're reaching out to long-lost sinners, till every island in the sea
   Knows about how Jesus came to die for you and me.

---

[2] Alexander J. Simpson, op. cit.

I have a small notebook full of Bible references of words that I believe the Lord has spoken about His work in Micronesia, as well as very personal promises for my family and me. Maybe I am like Ezekiel, seeing visions of impossible things—dry bones come to life! Ezekiel's vision has not been completely fulfilled yet. The "bones" that have gathered in the Promised Land are still not filled with the "breath" of the Holy Spirit (Ezek. 37:1–14).

I don't know whether I will live to see the fulfillment of all of God's promises. I suspect that some may only be fulfilled after my glorious Savior has returned to earth to reign as King of kings and Lord of lords. That's not my problem. The Sovereign Lord is the Promiser and the Fulfiller. I have only one responsibility—to keep my eyes focused on Him and my ears attentive to His voice.[3]

Meanwhile, I will continue to serve Him, believing that He delights in using small people who fully understand that all the glory belongs to Him. *"There is no limit to what God can do with a man providing he will not touch the glory."*[4]

Wherever the Lord sends me or whatever task He assigns me, I know that I will not be alone. A verse of Scripture and poem that were sent to me by someone thirty-five years ago eloquently express the words I hear Him speaking to me.

"As Thou Goest"

"As thou goest, step by step, I will open the way before thee."
—Prov. 4:12.

Child of My love, fear not the unknown morrow,
    dread not the new demand life makes of thee;
Thy ignorance doth hold no cause for sorrow
    since what thou knowest not is known to Me.
Thou canst not see today the hidden meaning
    of My command, but thou the light shall gain;
Walk on in faith, upon My promise leaning,
    and as thou goest all shall be made plain.

---

[3] See Principle #30, Appendix.
[4] Quoted by Mrs. Charles E. Cowman, *Streams in the Desert*, p. 212.

WALKING THE WAVES

One step thou seest—then go forward boldly.
    One step is far enough for faith to see.
Take that, and thy next duty shall be told thee,
    for step by step thy Lord is leading thee.
Stand not in fear, thy adversaries counting;
    dare every peril, save to disobey.
Thou shalt march on, all obstacles surmounting,
    for I, the Strong, will open up the way.
Wherefore, go gladly to the task assigned thee,
    having My promise, needing nothing more
Than just to know, where'er the future find thee,
    in all thy journeying I go before.

As I go, in my hand and heart will be the Living Word. I expect to hear God's voice from it. How could I ever go back to the old life after I have felt the thrill of "walking the waves" with Jesus?

"Thy way is in the sea, and Thy path in the great waters."— Psa. 77:19 (KJV). "When He leads us out by unexpected ways, off the strong solid land, out upon the changing seas, *then* we may expect to see *His ways.*"[5]

---

[5] Rev. C. A. Fox, quoted by Mrs. Charles E. Cowman, *Springs in the Valley*, p. 301.

APPENDIX

I have been urged by godly advisors to try to capsulize the principles or processes which have governed my experiences of "hearing the voice of God." I find this very difficult, because my "walking of the waves" has been so natural and unencumbered by rules and legalism. It has been nothing more than a total commitment to the hearing of God's voice, allowing Him, when He has chosen, to speak specific messages. However, in light of recent distortions of this truth within the Christian community, I have attempted to do as requested.

Principles
Which Have Emerged
As I Have Learned to "Hear" God Speak

1. The Lord often shows us His will through deep convictions of the heart or through circumstances; but most clearly and precisely through His Word.

2. Without faith in the personality and trustworthiness of God, we will never "hear" Him speak. A deep and total commitment to the Person of the Lord is what opens our hearts to His voice. It is not, as some people claim, "An emptying of our minds." I have never done that and never will, because I am aware of the many deceptive spirits abroad, as well as the fact of my own personal deceitfulness.

3. God speaks most often through our daily, faithful times with His Word—in Bible study, scripture memorization, the use of a daily devotional book, etc. I have never "hunted" for an answer to my question or for special guidance. That kind of search opens us to delusion. We must be willing to wait for God's timing, letting God be God!

WALKING THE WAVES

4. The Lord's special messages can bring pain. They are not always full of joy, promise, and victory. They may be warnings of judgment ahead.

5. Some of God's messages are only for the individual to whom they are spoken.

6. We can misinterpret what God says to us. Messages that we don't understand we need to leave in the Lord's hands, but continue to believe that what He has said He will accomplish in *His* time.

7. One of the proofs that it is the Lord who has spoken is the fulfillment of what He has said.

8. The Spirit often speaks in general rather than specific terms, but this is just as significant for our growth.

9. God knows when our requests for guidance come from a sincere desire and willingness to do what He indicates. I believe that He is sometimes "silent" because we have not yet obeyed His last word to us. When God knows that we are eager to obey whatever He indicates, He is eager to show us anything further that we need to know.

10. We need to have faith in God's Word even when it doesn't agree with what others are saying. We can safely leave it in the Lord's hands, knowing that He will reveal the truth in His time and way.

11. When we request guidance from the Father we must grant Him time to answer *when* He wants to and in the *way* He wants to. He is Almighty God, who reveals Himself only when He chooses. He is not a "vending machine" at our beck and call! To treat Him as such is blasphemous.

12. When the Lord has given us a special promise, it is our responsibility to hold it in our hearts, trusting the Author in the dark times when it seems that all has failed and the promise is false. "Tarry at the promise till God meets you there. He always returns by way of His promises."[1]

---

[1] Quoted by Mrs. Charles Cowman, *Streams in the Desert*, p. 140.

13. Trust seems to always come first, and full understanding later. If we insist on full understanding first, then we show that we are unwilling to trust our mighty, unseen God. We cannot expect Him to fully reveal Himself to those who question His veracity. "Faith and reality are not enemies. Faith is built upon the reality of divine revelation, evidences of divine fulfillment of promises, divine revelation in the natural world."[2]

14. Self-pity tends to turn us against God and toward ourselves, closing our ears to His voice. I have also found in my counseling that self-pity can lay us open to deceiving spirits and demonic visitations. It is rooted in rebellion against God and the circumstances He has elected to put us into.

15. We must believe that God is always "fair," and understand that He isn't obligated to explain Himself to us.

16. When the Father is silent, or we don't understand what He is doing, we must simply trust His perfect character.

17. We must be willing to accept God's call as irrevocable, and yet to know that as we obey His call, He will speak words of comfort and strength to us as He journeys with us.

18. Hearing the Spirit speak may be the precursor to pain and suffering, but commitment to His words and His will result in thanksgiving, peace, and joy in trouble.

19. Sometimes the Lord voices something to us which should not be shared with others. When He speaks, we need to find out from Him whether the information should be shared or not.

20. God's primary purpose in speaking to us is that we may know Him better. If we are wanting to "hear" Him only out of curiosity, to further our own ends, or to give us some kind of unique power, we quench the Spirit and silence the voice of the Almighty.

21. The Holy Spirit may speak directly to us, but He will never speak anything which does not line up with biblical

---

[2] Ron Susek, op. cit.

principles. His "voice" is always subject to confirmation from His written Word, and from the character of God as revealed in Scripture.

22. Sometimes we choose to deny that God has spoken because the message does not coincide with our plans. We also may invent a "word from God" to augment our plans. These are personal delusions of our flesh.

23. We don't have to "work deals" to assure that God's message will be fulfilled. He will carry out everything that He has truly spoken without our so-called assistance. Promises are fulfilled by God's sovereign commitment, not by our effort.

24. Discernment, with obedience to God, helps us to be able to recognize and identify the "other voices" that may speak to us.

25. Our commitment to the Lord's personal guidance will be tested by Him.

26. Listening to God entails the willingness to suffer and accept the hard lessons from Him.

27. When the Father calls us to a specific ministry and we respond in obedience, we can be sure that He will take care of the details and supply the financial and human support needed.

28. The Lord passes on His burdens to us, expecting us to accept them and act on them in prayer and ministry.

29. The Holy Spirit often puts prayers in our mouths directly from God's Word. Then we enter into the awesome partnership of praying His thoughts back to Him.

30. It dishonors the Lord when we doubt His ability to fulfill His promises. On the other hand, it shows serious disrespect when we try to force His hand to do something we believe He has promised. We must let God be God! He has the right to speak whenever He chooses, and to fulfill His words at His chosen time and in His chosen way.

This book was produced by the Christian Literature Crusade. We hope it has been helpful to you in living the Christian life. CLC is a literature mission with ministry in over 40 countries worldwide. If you would like to know more about us, or are interested in opportunities to serve with a faith mission, we invite you to write to:

Christian Literature Crusade
P.O. Box 1449
Fort Washington, PA 19034